THE DULUTH GRILL COOK BOOK

THE

DULUTH GRILL

COOK BOOK

WRITTEN BY **ROBERT LILLEGARD**

PHOTOGRAPHY BY **ROLF HAGBERG**

Duluth Grill Publishing
118 South 27th Avenue West
Duluth, MN 55806218-726-1150
info@DuluthGrill.com

THE DULUTH GRILL COOKBOOK

Printed in the United States of America
10 9 8 7 6 5 4 3 2 1 0 First Edition

ISBN-13: 978-0-9886112-0-7

All photos by Rolf Hagberg except where otherwise noted.
Designed by Kollath Graphic Design

TABLE *of* CONTENTS

LIST *of* RECIPES

CONDIMENTS & SAUCES

DRINKS

BREAKFAST

SOUPS AND STEWS

STARTERS

Vegetarian: ❦   Vegan: **V**   Gluten-Free: ★

SIDES

BIG HEARTY ENTREES

DESSERTS

DEDICATION

This book is dedicated to Alicia, who is my very favorite wife,
and who always lets me order for both of us at restaurants

AUTHOR'S NOTE

My first experience with the Duluth Grill was probably the same as a lot of people's. The "flexitarian" foods caught my eye (I decided to skip the Buffalo Tofu Strips), but the main thing that I noticed on the menu was the sheer variety. Do you want red flannel hash or regular hash browns? Would you like a roll as your side dish? Caramel or cinnamon? Or instead of a roll, how about French toast or a pancake, with lingonberry syrup or regular? You could also go for the regular toast with homemade peanut butter and jelly, or the fresh fruit or gluten-free pumpkin spice bread or Udi's gluten-free bagel or millet-chia toast. And don't worry. If you don't see something you like, it's easy to make substitutions.

When my brother wanted a Goober Burger (a burger topped with a fried egg and peanut butter), we knew he stood a good chance of getting one at the Grill. Our server was surprised,

but the order went through. And if you want a caramel roll at dinner, well, there are no guarantees — but I bet you'll be able to work something out.

You might have noticed that I haven't mentioned anything about the whole fresh/local/sustainable approach. That's because, like any restaurant, the most important thing about Duluth Grill is the food. And while Tom Hanson is certainly a leader in farm-to-table cooking, he's also a good cook. The recipes here provide plenty of delicious variety, from the first bite of pancakes in the morning to the last bit of banana cream pie at night.

And those Buffalo Tofu Strips I shied away from on my first visit? They're actually pretty good.

Happy Reading,
Robert

A WORD *from* TOM & JAIMA

It is been said when you love what you do you'll never work a day in your life. Well, I can tell you we love what we do, but it still feels like work. My wife and I have both been in the business since the late 70s. I often think the restaurant business picked us versus us focusing on the question, "what do I want to be when I grow up", and pursuing a career. Our kids have been in the business directly or indirectly in one form or another. They've experienced the dedication it takes to work through every weekend, holidays, and long endless days rolling together into 100 hour weeks. So we ask ourselves—why do we do it? Our business has gone far beyond supporting ourselves. Our son Louis and his wife Ashley have dedicated their careers to this business and started raising a family of future restaurateurs. Jeff Petcoff is like a son to us and has grown up in our family being best friends with Louis and with us since he was seventeen. Now he's the general manager and has a charming family of his own. Dan and Whitney LeFebvre met here and now dedicate their careers to our business. We have a staff of more than eighty employees that rely on our success. That's one more reason we do what we do.

Another big reason is our guests. This summer we fed almost a thousand guests a day, but there was one guest I'll never forget. I was in the kitchen, probably scrambling to get an order ready or answering a phone call, when one of our new servers came in and told Jaima and me about the

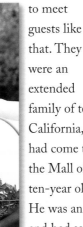

Tom & Jaima Hanson

family she was serving.

"You've gotta meet this family," she said. "They came all the way here to eat our food and try our pie."

So we went out in to the dining room, because there's always time to meet guests like that. They were an extended family of ten from Sacramento, California, and they told us they had come to Minnesota to visit the Mall of America. But their ten-year old son had other ideas. He was an avid Food Network fan and had seen the Duluth Grill on *Diners, Drive-Ins, and Dives*. So he persuaded his family to rent an Econoline van, drive up to Duluth, and eat with us. He loved the food and the pie. We shook his hand, Jaima gave him a hug, we gave him a signed Duluth Grill T-shirt, and they took a picture with us to be included in their family's log of travel adventures. They went on their way (after grandpa bought Duluth Grill shirts for all the girls too), and left calling out goodbyes as if we were part of their family. I could tell he had a good time, and his grandmother proved it with an extensive letter expressing a grandmother's gratitude for making Matthew's vacation special. WOW!

"Expect more people from Sacramento coming your

Duluth Grill was featured on the Food Network's *Diners, Drive-ins, and Dives.*

way because we are shouting your praises daily," she wrote. "And speaking for our family…. WE WILL BE BACK!"

People like that family come out to our restaurant all the time, and they love our food. So they ask us for our recipes: "Oh, this is so great, how do you make this?"

Ten times a week people ask how we make our ketchup, soups, lasagna or desserts. We've always given it to them but we feel we can do better than handing out one recipe at a time.

Thinking about writing a cookbook and actually doing it is more challenging for us than one may think. Writing this simple letter was enough. We work at a vigorous pace and love it. Sitting down is not in either my wife's or my nature. We were talking about it over coffee and during walks to the restaurant. That's how it just came about. Customers asked, "when's a cookbook coming out?" We said "soon" but we didn't actually have a plan.

During this time, I started to get to know Robert Lillegard. Robert has been published in the *New York Times* and many other national publications and has a rising list of accomplishments. He had written articles about us for *Duluth-Superior Magazine* and other

"We hope to inspire future cooks to work with simple ingredients, play with food, and use clean products to get great results"

The extended Duluth Grill family (from left to right): François Medion, Valerie Bigelow, Tom Hanson, Elliot Bigelow, Jaima Hanson, Parker & Ashley Hanson, Peyton Hanson and Louis Hanson.

publications, and he did a good job telling our story. I thought it was great as far as where he was published. And an article he wrote for *Foodservice News* actually had some information about my restaurant that even I didn't know. When he called me last summer to get some information about our urban farm, I asked what he thought about working together on a cookbook.

He agreed and we got started. Robert brought in some top talent— photographer Rolf Hagberg, who has done high level work for big companies, and designer Rick Kollath, who has designed and published nature field guides sold all over the upper Midwest. As you can imagine, it wasn't cheap. Do you ever have that moment where your mechanic tells you how much it will cost? And it sort of hits you: this is going to hurt. There have been a few moments like that with this book. It made Jaima a little nervous. Me? I'm probably nervous about a lot of things but then I just do them anyhow.

The thing is, we're about quality. I have to say that I don't really work for money—I work for the return on the investment. I care about what the long-term returns are. We want this book to be something that when people look at it, they can be proud of it. And it's a lot more satisfying to make something that will last. Every recipe in this book was broken down mathematically, reformulated for home user-friendly portions, and (with the exception of a few we added at the end) cooked by one of a few expert home cooks. Each dish was tasted before it was approved for print. Our thanks to Darlene Seelos, Sarah Witzig, Kristina Hayes, and Angie Peterson for their dedication in making this a book you can use. Although our recipes are unique to our restaurant, we hope to inspire future cooks to work with simple ingredients, play with food, and use clean products to get great results. Like Hippocrates said, "Let your food be your medicine and your medicine be your food."

Our moment in this industry is brief. We might be here twenty years, twenty-five years. But with this cookbook, we have something people can look at fifty years from now and be a useful guide in the kitchen. Clean, healthy eating will always be in style.

Jaima compares our dedication to serve to one of our favorite bands. The BoDeans are an indie rock band from Waukesha, Wisconsin and we went down to a show a few years ago. It was such an interactive show everyone really got into it.

"They make you feel like you can sing any one of their songs," Jaima says. "You dance, you feel the music in you. Even Tom danced."

To which I'll add: no comment.

Anyway, Jaima says a restaurant can be a lot like a rock band. Rock fans will buy rock T-shirts, and our fans buy our T-shirts and coffee mugs. We try to remember what moves people to support us. People are fascinated with a stage show, and we put on a good one. All day our servers are weaving through crowds of people, getting right up next to each other but not colliding, and holding huge trays of food without spilling. You can hear our kitchen blurting out commands and dishes clanging from our dedicated crew in the "dish-pit". Some of our customers just sit there and watch, admiring each move our staff makes.

Just like the BoDeans draw people in to their shows, we'd like people to feel connected to the restaurant. After being in the business, we wanted our food to be more meaningful. We wanted to be in control of the outcome of the product. The cookbook is a way of breaking down the process so our customers can get that same kind of passion in their own kitchen.

And that's true even if they're far, far away. A couple of years ago, a man wrote to me from the Virgin Islands, saying he had seen me on *Diners, Drive-Ins, and Dives*. He asked for our banana cream pie recipe, which you'll find on page 118 of this book. I sent it over and asked him to send a photo if he was successful. I got the photo, it looked great! I can just imagine this guy on the beach by the palm trees with a piña colada, a hammock, and our banana cream pie. Our fans are our friends too.

So, we're proud to present you with our cookbook. But before I conclude here, I've got something to say. I told Kay Biga that when I wrote my memoirs, I would be sure to thank her. I'm not sure I'll ever write my memoirs—especially now that I see what an undertaking a book is—so this will have to do.

Kay owned this restaurant before we did, and she laid a path for us to be successful. For the first five years, she provided us with a turn-key lease. We were able to walk into the restaurant and be in business with the supplies on hand—up to and including the dishes and silverware. When it came time to buy at the end of five years, she even tried to help us get a loan. Kay, thanks for your help.

And thanks to the rest of you, too. Without our staff, without our guests, we wouldn't be in business at all, much less putting together a cookbook. So here's to the future, and to all of you. **DG**

THREE-DAY MEAL PLANS

GLUTEN-FREE

Manager Jeff Petcoff, owner Tom Hanson, manager Louis Hanson, and writer Robert Lillegard strike a pose for the annual *Men Standing In Gardens* calendar.

TESTED BY HOME COOKS

We wanted this cookbook to be easy and usable by the home cook. So, we got help from four local home cooks—Darlene Seelos, Angie Peterson, Sarah Witzig, and Kristina Hayes. Each took on the task of converting recipes from their large, restaurant-sized format to a smaller make-at-home size. With the exception of a few recipes added at the very end of the process — recipes Tom personally vouches for — they tested each one. So when you cook a recipe from this book, know that you're not the first!

There's some controversy about this, but the most credible theory about the early history of the Duluth Grill involves a highway rest area, a pregnant woman, and a lot of soap operas. The restaurant started as Highway Host in June of 1970, and served burgers and fries to the truckers passing through. In 1991, a manager took maternity leave and watched a lot of *General Hospital*. As managers sometimes do, she called the owners and suggested a name change. The gang on *General Hospital* kept meeting up at the Port Charles Grill, so why not call the restaurant the Duluth Grill? The owners liked the name and it stuck.

But in spite of the catchy new name, the Duluth Grill closed in 2001. Tom and Jaima Hanson cashed out their 401k and leased the building with two business partners. The partners owned five Embers restaurants between, and at that time Embers was offering to waive start-up costs to anyone opening a sixth location. So, with $12,000 and a handshake, the Duluth Grill Embers was born.

Six months later, the partnership dissolved. Fortunately, everyone stayed out of court, and the Hansons ended up keeping the restaurant. One fateful morning, they ran out of pancake mix and decided to whip up their own. It tasted better than the official Embers-approved mix, and it was cheaper too. This is when things started to change. They began adding new menu items like homemade lasagna, along with vegetarian, gluten-free, and local options.

"If you put edamame on the menu in Embers in 2006, would it

Embers®

sell? No," Tom says. "So I called them Soybean Snackers and they sold like crazy."

Meanwhile, Embers was losing franchisees left and right and not offering much support to the ones who remained. So in 2008, the Duluth Grill officially broke ties. They joined the Sustainable Twin Ports project and took on a new direction.

HOW DID THE DULUTH GRILL GET STARTED?

"We started getting this young, vibrant group," Tom says. "We've mainstreamed organic dishes in a restaurant everyone can enjoy."

By the time the gardens came in 2009, the Hansons were already working with many local growers. Every year, they're adding new projects. With fruit trees in their yard, rooftop gardens and beehives at the restaurant, a full time farm manager, and their own small fish farm, the future is looking strong. But it all started with the simple step of making their own food.

"In the beginning it was to try to be in control of our own destiny rather than trying to serve mediocre food better," Tom says. "You realize there's really no winning that battle. So we took it in a different direction of what we wanted to do." **DG**

The Embers crew: Tom, Jeff Petcoff & Jaima

This menu was found under a booth when Tom and Jaima bought the restaurant in 2001.

DELICIOUS DINNERS

SIDE ORDERS

SENIOR SPECIALS

THE PEOPLE BEHIND THE FOOD

MARK AND TERRI THELL:
4 QUARTERS HOLDING FAMILY FARM IN WRENSHALL

The Duluth Grill uses between 500 and 600 pounds of beef every three weeks, and it all comes from Mark and Terri Thell. Tom describes them as every bit the classic farmer couple, with big work ethics and plenty to say once you get them going.

"Terri, she was just awesome," Tom says. "You can tell she's a grandma full in and full out. She has grandchildren of her own, talks about them all the time. She'll bring in 600 pounds of beef like it's nobody's business. She's this tiny little lady, too."

> *"You can tell she's a grandma full in and full out."*

Terri and Mark Thell at home on the range.

PHOTOS BY JEFF PETCOFF

While Terri is hauling enormous amounts of beef around, Mark is out with the cattle. Tom says he's dedicated and hardworking, with a good reputation and a lot on his mind.

"Mark is quiet, yet will keep talking," Tom says. "He knows what he's doing, he will think things out. He almost goes into more than what you want to know."

Ultimately, Tom says, what drives both of them is a sense of pride in their work. You won't find anonymous steaks slapped into a plastic wrapper, but people who live and breathe farming.

"I guess I can't describe it but you can sense it when someone's proud of something," Tom says. "You ask [Mark] questions about ideas and you can tell, just his look and the pride he has when he talks about his cattle. **DG**

THE PEOPLE BEHIND THE FOOD

DAVE ROGOTZKE: SIMPLE GIFTS IN DULUTH

Duluthian Dave Rogotzke provides the maple syrup and salmon for the Duluth Grill, and Tom met him shortly before the maple syrup harvest. He was invited out to see what Dave calls the "sugar shack", which turned out to be located way out in the woods. After driving past the driveway once or twice (it's notoriously hard to find), Tom turned up a gravel road and was promptly blown away.

"What he calls a 'sugar shack' is this gorgeous looking house," Tom says. "You walk in there and there are these kettles for boiling and these tanks for storing. You realize that it's not a shack, it's an operation—and yet it's one guy."

The sap process runs from mid-March to mid-April and the Rogotzke family has 5000 taps, which allow them to produce several hundred gallons a year. The Duluth Grill alone buys between 380 and 420 gallons annually. It's pricey, but quite popular with guests—Tom says he's seen at least one older gentleman eat it straight from the bottle with a spoon.

But Dave's popular with the younger set as

He's allowed his own daughters to experience what every little girl dreams of: commercial salmon fishing.

well. He does several tours of the operation each year to let school kids see the whole process, from sap to syrup. Plus, he's allowed his own daughters to experience what every little girl dreams of: commercial salmon fishing.

The daddy-daughter salmon trips with Katie and Leah have been more of a recent development, but Dave himself has been fishing in Bristol Bay, Alaska for over twenty-five years. Since it's wild caught, the King and Sockeye salmon aren't artificially colored or tainted with high levels of PCB like farm-raised salmon often are.

Dave's wife, an ob-gyn doctor, also has a connection to the Duluth Grill, though it's a little more oblique.

"Not only is Dave a neat guy, his wife actually delivered Ashley and Louis' second child," Tom says. "I guess there's more of a connection in these little connections and you realize we're not too far off from each other. DG

PHOTO BY JEFF PETCOFF

Condiments & Sauces

STRAWBERRY JAM

Jam is not an exact science, so feel free to play around with different fruits and use more or less sugar as desired.

INGREDIENTS:

1 pound organic fresh or frozen strawberries

2 cups sugar

2 tablespoons lemon juice

DIRECTIONS:

- If using frozen berries let them thaw completely.
- Mash berries with a potato masher or pulse in a blender.
- Place berries, sugar and lemon juice in a heavy saucepan and bring to 220 degrees using a candy thermometer.
- Watch closely so it does not boil over or scorch.
- Place in refrigerator and chill completely. Yields 3 cups.

PEANUT BUTTER

Once Tom realized how simple homemade peanut butter was, it was a no-brainer to start making it for the restaurant.

INGREDIENTS:

1 pound roasted peanuts, no salt

4 tablespoons butter, softened

¼ cup Canola oil

2 tablespoons honey

pinch of salt

DIRECTIONS:

- If peanuts are salted do not add salt to the recipe.
- Place all ingredients in a food processor and blend until creamy. Yields 2 cups.

RASPBERRY VINAIGRETTE

A classic raspberry vinaigrette is delicious with a salad of field greens, especially when you add sliced almonds and feta cheese.

INGREDIENTS:

¾ cup raspberries

½ cup cider vinegar

2 tablespoons maple syrup

½ teaspoon Dijon mustard (some brands may not be gluten free)

¼ cup olive oil

¼ teaspoon salt

⅛ teaspoon white pepper

DIRECTIONS:

- In a food processor mix berries, vinegar and maple syrup until smooth.
- Add mustard, salt and pepper; blend for 30 seconds.
- Keeping the processor running slowly add the oil. This should take 1-2 minutes. Refrigerate. Yields about 1½ cups.

MANGO VINAIGRETTE

This taste of the tropics is excellent with a simple salad or as a marinade for pork or chicken.

INGREDIENTS:

½ cup mango puree (about 1 mango)

½ cup rice wine vinegar

¼ cup sesame oil

½ tablespoon crushed red pepper flakes

1 tablespoon honey

DIRECTIONS:

- Combine mango, vinegar, honey and red pepper flakes in a food processor.
- Keeping the processor running slowly add the oil (this should take about a minute or two just to add the oil).
- Pour into a jar and refrigerate until ready to use. Yields about 1 cup.

BALSALMIC VINAIGRETTE

A good balsamic vinaigrette is simplicity itself. The Duluth Grill's version has just four ingredients and a clean, pure taste.

INGREDIENTS:

¼ cup Balsamic vinegar

¼ teaspoon Dijon mustard (some brands may not be gluten free)

1 tablespoon red onion, diced

½ cup olive oil

DIRECTIONS:

* In a food processor blend vinegar, mustard and red onion until smooth.
* Keeping the processor running slowly add the oil (this should take about a minute or two just to add the oil). Yields ¾ cup.

ROSEMARY VINAIGRETTE

Give your salads a Mediterranean flair with this elegant dressing, which also works as a marinade.

INGREDIENTS:

⅓ cup rice wine vinegar

¾ teaspoon Dijon mustard (some brands may not be gluten free)

1 ½ tablespoons red onion

⅔ cup olive oil

1-2 sprigs fresh rosemary (leaves only)

DIRECTIONS:

* In a food processor add vinegar, mustard, red onion and fresh rosemary.
* Keeping the processor running, slowly add the oil. This should take about a minute or two just to add the oil.
* Pour into a jar and refrigerate until ready to use. Yields about 1 cup.

FRENCH DRESSING

Ou est le bibliotheque? Tap in to your high school French and enjoy a delicious salad at the same time. *Oh la la!*

INGREDIENTS:

½ cup minced onion

1 ¼ cup extra virgin olive oil

¾ cup cider vinegar

1 cup sugar

¼ cup ketchup

1 tablespoon balsamic vinegar

½ tablespoon salt

½ tablespoon Dijon mustard

½ tablespoon smoky paprika

1 tablespoon garlic powder

1 tablespoon celery seed

DIRECTIONS:

* In a food processor or blender, blend onion and olive oil together until smooth.

* Add the rest of the ingredients and blend until completely incorporated.

* Label, date, refrigerate. Yields about 1 quart.

RANCH DRESSING

In the Midwest, this goes with everything from chicken nuggets to pizza.

INGREDIENTS:

2 cups mayo

1 tablespoon parsley

1 tablespoon seasoned salt

½ tablespoon onion powder

1 cup buttermilk

½ tablespoon black pepper

¼ tablespoon garlic powder

¼ tablespoon thyme

DIRECTIONS:

* In a blender or food processor add mayo and seasonings, mix until smooth.

* Slowly add buttermilk while mixing and continue to mix until smooth.

* Label, date, refrigerate. Yields 3 cups.

French Dressing

Blue Cheese Dressing

Ranch Dressing

Huny-Rika Sauce

Pesto Sauce

BLUE CHEESE DRESSING

Local magazine editor Wendy Webb says she'd be happy to bathe in this dressing. It's the perfect complement for spicy Buffalo wings.

INGREDIENTS:

1 cup mayonnaise

⅓ cup Bleu Cheese crumbles

1 tablespoon grated Parmesan cheese

dash white pepper

4 tablespoons buttermilk

½ teaspoon granulated garlic

DIRECTIONS:

- Put mayonnaise into a mixing bowl.
- Add granulated garlic, white pepper and Parmesan cheese and mix thoroughly.
- Add buttermilk.
- Add crumbled Bleu cheese and mix thoroughly. Refrigerate until use. Yields about 1 ½ cups.

PESTO SAUCE

Pesto is traditionally prepared with a mortar and pestle (hence the name), but this tasty sauce can be made more easily in a modern food processor.

INGREDIENTS:

3 ounces fresh basil

¼ cup minced garlic

¾ cups olive oil

½ cup shredded Parmesan

1 ½ teaspoon sea salt

DIRECTIONS:

Blend all ingredients except the olive oil in a food processor. Slowly add the olive oil until the consistency is smooth and well blended.

HUNY-RIKA SAUCE (AKA "Z-SAUCE")

Manager Jeff Petcoff spent several hours alphabetizing all of the Duluth Grill's recipes in a binder. Then, Tom proudly announced we had added a delicious new sauce that would be going in the cookbook. Jeff promptly named it "Z-Sauce" and filed it at the very back.

INGREDIENTS:

1 cup mayonnaise

½ cup honey

¼ cup lemon juice

¾ tablespoon Smokey paprika

¾ teaspoon sea salt

¾ teaspoon cinnamon

¾ teaspoon cayenne pepper

DIRECTIONS:

In a food processor add all ingredients and mix thoroughly until smooth. Pour into a jar and refrigerate until ready to use. This is good as a dipping sauce for sweet potato fries or as a salad dressing Yields about 1 ½ cups.

CHIPOTLE PECANS

Made with orange juice, brown sugar, and a hint of chipotle, these nuts are great on their own or as an ingredient in salads.

INGREDIENTS:

1 tablespoons orange juice

1 egg white

2 cups pecans

1 tablespoon brown sugar

1 teaspoon salt

½ teaspoon chipotle pepper (ground)

DIRECTIONS:

- In a mixing bowl combine orange juice and egg white. Add pecans.
- In a separate bowl combine brown sugar, salt and chipotle pepper. Add to pecan mixture, toss well.
- Spray a sheet pan with cooking spray and spread pecans evenly on it.
- Bake at 225 degrees for 1 hour.
- Allow to cool. Store in an airtight container.
- Yields 2 cups.

SALAD SAVVY

One of the best things about salads is the variety. If you mix up your ingredients day to day, you'll never get bored. Here are four salads we serve at the Grill.

Big Chicken Burrito Bowl: *It's like a burrito salad! Fresh cilantro & lime seasoned wild rice and chipotle BBQ sauce (similar recipe on page 85), topped with spicy beans, corn, sautéed onions & green peppers, Pico de Gallo (59 in intro to salsa recipe), shredded cheese, fiesta chicken, lettuce, tomato, sour cream, guacamole (58), and fresh salsa (59).*

Big Veggie Salad: *Fresh greens topped with broccoli, Bay Produce tomatoes, green pepper, avocado, red onions, dried cranberries, toasted chipotle pecans (10), and alfalfa sprouts. Topped with bleu cheese crumbles and served with your choice of dressing.*

Smoked Salmon Salad: *Fresh greens topped with Northern Waters smoked salmon, Danish Havarti cheese with dill, fresh cilantro, Pico de Gallo (59 in intro to salsa recipe), fresh avocados, sweet brined onions and fresh bell peppers with roasted red pepper vinaigrette (81).*

Cobb Salad: *Fresh greens with grilled chicken, Applewood smoked bacon, Kalamata olives, tomatoes, blue cheese crumbles, fresh avocado, and hard boiled egg.*

CARAMEL SAUCE

Next to "yummy" in the dictionary, you'll find a picture of Caramel Sauce.

INGREDIENTS:

1 pound (2 -¼ cups) sugar

½ cup water

1-½ teaspoons lemon juice

1-½ cups heavy cream

DIRECTIONS:

- Add sugar, water and lemon juice together in a pan and cook over medium high heat.

- Cook until mixture turns golden brown. No need to stir constantly, about 10 minutes of boiling.

- In a separate pan bring heavy cream to a boil. Take pan off heat.

- Slowly add cream to the caramel sauce and stir together. Start with just a drip of cream as mixture will bubble up a lot. Be careful not to get splattered. You might want to wear oven mitts for this part.

- Return sauce to heat and cook until sauce is full incorporated. (Only a few minutes). Yields 2 ¾ cups.

CHOCOLATE SAUCE

While a bowl of this makes for a perfectly respectable dinner, there's no reason to stop there. Fill a Nalgene with it and take it camping, pour it into a trough for the kids at your next family reunion, or swap out your IV bag for a Zip-Loc full.

INGREDIENTS:

½ cup butter

½ cup cocoa

1 cup and 2 tablespoons sugar

1 cup milk

½ cup chocolate chips

DIRECTIONS:

- Melt butter. Add cocoa and stir until smooth.

- Add sugar and stir until smooth. Slowly stir in the milk.

- Add chocolate chips when it starts to boil.

- Boil for 30 minutes while stirring. Chocolate sauce shouldn't be runny. Yields 1 ¾ cups.

Drinks

LEMONADE

When life gives you organic cane sugar, make lemonade. No, wait. When life gives you water, make lemonade. No, that's not how it goes either. At any rate, this is a refreshing drink you can enhance even further by adding crushed berries to taste (you may have to add a little more sugar if the berries aren't sweet enough).

INGREDIENTS:

2 cups fresh squeezed lemon juice

2 cups organic cane sugar

2 cups water

DIRECTIONS:

- Heat lemon juice, sugar and water to a minimal boil, with water just hot enough to dissolve the sugar granules completely.

- After sugar is dissolved, pull from heat and add 8 more cups of water to mix.

- Place in a 1 gallon pitcher, chill completely, and serve. Yields 12 cups.

THE HEALTHY ELVIS

With healthy fat from peanut butter, fiber from oats, banana, and chia seeds, and creamy yogurt and coconut milk, this is truly breakfast in a glass.

INGREDIENTS:

2 tablespoons peanut butter

1 banana

½ cup old fashioned oats

1 tablespoon chia seeds

½ cup coconut milk

½ cup vanilla yogurt

1 tablespoon honey

½ cup of ice

DIRECTIONS:

Place all ingredients in a blender and blend to a creamy smooth consistency. Serve immediately. Yields a 16-ounce smoothie.

GREEN GODDESS OF GOODNESS

Spinach and spirulina in a smoothie. Consistently creamy chia and coconut. Bodacious banana in a blender. Okay, we're done with the alliteration now.

INGREDIENTS:

½ apple

1 peach

½ banana

1 cup spinach

1 teaspoon spirulina

1 tablespoon chia seed

¾ cup coconut milk

DIRECTIONS:

Place all ingredients in a blender and blend to a creamy smooth consistency. Serve immediately. Yields a 16-ounce smoothie.

Do it Ahead of Time

*Sometimes it's the simplest things that keep people from
making healthy choices. Make mornings easy by preparing
these smoothies ahead of time. Prepare all the ingredients
(except the milk and yogurt) in one sitting and separate
out into individual sized Zip Loc bags, then place in the
freezer. When you wake up, just place in the blender with
milk and yogurt and blend. You can get a month's worth
of smoothies ready all at once—it's healthy and fast!*

ORANGE YOU GLAD

Knock knock.

Who's there?

Banana.

Banana who?

Knock knock.

Who's there?

Banana.

Banana who?

Knock knock.

Who's there?

Orange.

Orange who?

Orange you glad I didn't say banana?

INGREDIENTS:

½ peach

4 baby carrots

1 dime size slice of fresh peeled ginger

1 tablespoon honey

¾ cup coconut milk

½ cup vanilla yogurt

DIRECTIONS:

Place all ingredients in a blender and blend until a creamy
smooth consistency. Serve immediately. Yields a 16-ounce
smoothie.

PURPLE BERRY BLAST

Strawberries, blueberries, and blackberries can all
be picked locally, so this smoothie is a good way
to use up summer's bounty.

INGREDIENTS:

5 strawberries

¼ cup blackberries

¼ cup blueberries

½ banana

1 cup kefir

1 tablespoon honey

DIRECTIONS:

Place all ingredients in a blender and blend to smooth.
Pour into a glass and serve immediately.

Yields a 16-ounce smoothie.

HOT COCOA

When it's winter and you're in love, there's nothing like a warm mug of hot cocoa. Of course, when you break up hot cocoa can ease the pain. Then again, when you're not really in love OR heartbroken, hot cocoa's delicious as well. Essentially what we're saying is there's never a bad time for hot cocoa.

INGREDIENTS:

½ cup cocoa powder

½ cup malted milk powder

½ cup chocolate sauce (see page 11)

8 cups skim milk

Whipped cream

DIRECTIONS:

• In a mixing bowl mix dry ingredients with a whisk.

• Place 8 cups of milk on stove in a large enough pot to hold all ingredients.

• Heat the milk to 160 degrees and add the dry ingredients and the chocolate sauce. Mix well.

• Take off the oven and serve immediately in your favorite coffee mug. Top with whipped cream. Yields about 8 servings.

AN URBAN FARM &
GARDENS ON THE ROOF

It's a sunny but cold day in June, and farm manager François Medion is straddling a rain barrel. He's showing his niece Olivia, who just arrived from France for a three month stay, how to saw it in half with a jigsaw. He's wearing work boots and a dirty T-shirt that says "When the world wearies and ceases to satisfy, there is always the garden." She's dressed a little less ruggedly, with Chuck Taylors, dark makeup, and a cigarette tucked behind her ear. But together, they're building a rooftop garden.

He leans a ladder against the side of the restaurant and we climb up. The black roof has several small pools of water, evidence of the terrible drainage. There are already a few half-barrels up there, ready to serve as containers for plants. What's not yet clear is how many the roof can hold.

"I'd be happy to have an engineer or architect telling me," François says. "I'll put as many barrels as I can."

It's always awkward when your

birthday dinner is interrupted by the roof caving in. To prevent those ceiling-tiles-in-the-cake moments, François and Olivia will be using a blend of ultra-light materials instead of normal potting soil. Coir (made from coconut fiber), vermiculite (a lightweight clay), and perlite (a lightweight volcanic glass) will keep the weight down and the roof protected.

The roof will host squash and pumpkin plants, vine crops that will spread out on their own. Watering is a simple matter of using condensation from the air conditioner and waiting for the rain to fall. When the roof is covered with plants, it will help cool the building below, saving on energy costs. Then, in fall, the squash and pumpkin will be harvested for the restaurant.

But the roof has more than just a handful of vine crops. After a bear took out the Duluth Grill's beehives, they moved them up top. Two little hives provide some of the restaurant's honey, but both zoning ordinances and the strong winds

Bear safe: beehives on the roof

coming off the lake have given François reason to worry.

"Potentially, the bees are illegal," François says. "Hopefully they stick around and don't swarm and take off."

François himself is no stranger to taking off and moving on. He grew up on a cognac-and-dairy farm in France, and later moved to Paris. He ended up doing circus-style car-on-fire stunts for a theatre group of former American inmates. When the show was over, they gave him a one-way ticket to America. He ended up in a ghetto in Newark, New Jersey, and still didn't speak any English.

Things got worse with his friends, so he quit and began waiting tables at a high-class French restaurant in New York City. The money was good, but he spent freely and was constantly broke. He got a fresh start in the Midwest, where he lived in a tepee (he ate at his job and showered at the gym). After years of landscaping work, he ran into Tom Hanson at a sustainability event and a friendship was born.

But it wasn't until a conference in Milwaukee in February 2010 that the two began to work together. Tom, his wife Jaima, and François learned about the idea of urban farming, where people in Milwaukee grew their own produce on small plots of land. As the group travelled home, Jaima realized there was a perfect garden spot just a mile away from the restaurant. Her daughter and son in law owned a little house on West 13th Street, and it was possible they'd be willing to sell. Hours after the sun had set, Tom made a plan.

"We gotta go see," Tom said.

The ever-prudent Jaima said it wasn't the best time. They could easily visit their daughter later that week, or even the next day, but not right then.

"It's 11 at night," she said. "We're going to wake up the neighbors."

"Oh, we gotta go see," Tom replied.

So they did. And there, as the moonlight glistened on the snow, the dream was born. Tom and Jaima bought the house from their daughter (who wanted to move to the Twin Cities anyway) and started their own little farm.

By the time I visit, the farm has come a long way from that snowy yard. François says I can ride with him to check it out, so I climb inside a big white pickup truck. There are two straw hats on the dashboard and a notebook and a chunk of galangal root on the seat. But the real action is happening in the driver's seat, where François is driving with one hand and gesturing with the other. Taro roots, he gestures, are about this big. The leaves are about this big.

I quickly find out that one hand on the wheel is a maximum for François, who's teaching me valuable lessons about both edge-of-your-seat driving and the ancient Incas.

"They have domesticated—I don't know how many thousands of root crops," he says, gesturing with both hands as the truck barrels down the highway. "We should be trying to expand the range of things we can grow here, and the diversity."

That diversity is already on display at the farm. A normal-sized lot is crammed full of flowers, herbs, and produce, and a big hoop house contains seedlings and a giant fish tank. There are rows of kale, beets, leeks, and celery, and also less conventional vegetables.

Lovage, a leafy perennial that tastes like a supercharged version of celery, hangs in a shed. Along the side of the yard, there's brightly colored strawberry blight, with leaves like spinach and a mildly sweet red fruit. François also likes hardy kiwi, a variety grown in Korea and Siberia that bears small fruits that look like grapes on the outside and the more common hairy kiwi on the inside. There are also local

> *"It's kind of ridiculous that people spend hours and hours a year grooming and trimming grass with zero return on that except that you have a green lawn. Having gardens in my yard, it's less work than cutting my grass."*

weeds like wild amaranth, purslane, and lamb's quarters (a relative of quinoa).

"Plants like this have something domesticated plants don't have," François says. "One of the ideas is to grow something that would be prohibitively expensive to get that nobody else has."

It looks rather odd, all these plants crammed together with terracing and a hoop house. But according to Tom, he's just bringing things back to a more natural state. If you have a yard, he says, you might as well use it.

"It's kind of ridiculous that people spend hours and hours a year grooming and trimming grass with zero return on that except that you have a green lawn," Tom says. "Having gardens in my yard, it's less work than cutting my grass."

Indeed, the aquaponics system practically runs itself. Inside the hoop house, there's a fish tank that will be able to hold 4,600 gallons of water and a school of fish. As with any fish tank, effluents from the fish will collect in the tank. They're toxic to fish, but essential food for plants. A pump will send the water to a top platform filled with gravel and plants, and then filter down and through a second layer. The plant layers will serve as giant filters, cleaning the water and providing food at the same time. François says they'll probably start with an Amazonian fish called the pacu.

"The beauty of the pacu is that they are voracious like piranhas, but vegetarian," François says.

François hopes to feed them with used vegetable matter from the restaurant, creating an elegant cycle and reducing waste at the same time. It's not the first time the restaurant has supported the farm. Old Stoneyfield Organic Yogurt containers now hold seedlings at the farm. The restaurant also plans to burn used fryer oil in a generator at the restaurant and sell the electricity back to the power company to help pay for the electricity used at the farm.

It's a sophisticated system, and it works. While no one is keeping track of exactly how much produce the farm and gardens yield each year, together there are roughly 6,000 square feet of growing space.

"But that's not counting the roof," François says. **DG**

GROWING UP IN A RESTAURANT

The old joke in the restaurant industry is that you only have to work half days—just twelve hours a day. But there's plenty of truth behind that little witticism. The Duluth Grill is open fourteen hours a day, seven days a week, and someone's got to be there to staff it. Louis Hanson, who was sixteen when his parents bought the restaurant, says it can put a drain on family time.

"They're gone all the time, that's about it." Louis says. "My mom didn't work as much as my dad, but you kind of learn to accept what it takes to run a restaurant."

His sister, who recently moved to the Twin Cities with her husband, worked for years as a server. His older brother used to help out, but ultimately found the industry wasn't for him. Louis says that's actually par for the course.

"The thing is, some people just aren't cut out for the restaurant industry. It's fast paced, it's demanding, it's hot, you've got people coming in at you all the time."

"The thing is, some people just aren't cut out for the restaurant industry," Louis says. "It's fast paced, it's demanding, it's hot, you've got people coming in at you all the time."

But Louis is following in his father's footsteps, working 50-plus hours a week at the restaurant. His wife Ashley serves a couple of days a week, but with a five year old and a two year old to take care of, she mostly stays home.

"I would recommend that anyone with kids not work in the restaurant business," Louis says. "You're just gone a lot. It's good to have a wife or a significant other that is at home with them and can provide a stable family style."

Tom says that as the family grows, it's causing him to think more about his ethics as a businessman. While making a profit is one thing, it's ultimately more important to do things the right way.

"I look at my grandkids now and think 'what kind of a businessperson do I want to represent to them?'" Tom says. "Money is coming into us and we're finding that it is pretty lucrative doing what we're doing. But we started on the basis of just trying to be good." **DG**

Breakfast

PANCAKE BATTER

2004 is a year that will forever live in pancake infamy. On a busy morning, the Duluth Grill Embers staff found themselves completely out of pancake batter. To fill the demand, they quickly whipped up a batch of their own. It was cheaper than the stuff Embers wanted them to use, and also tasted better. Tom and Jaima began to wonder why they didn't make more themselves, and a legend was born.

INGREDIENTS:

Dry Mix:

1 cup whole wheat flour

1 cup white flour

¾ cups sugar

2 teaspoons baking soda

1 tablespoon and 2-¾ teaspoon baking powder

2-¾ teaspoons salt

1 tablespoon and 1-¾ teaspoon cornstarch

Batter:

Dry mix from above

1 pint buttermilk

3 eggs

¼ cup melted butter

DIRECTIONS:

- Mix dry ingredients in large bowl.
- In separate bowl, mix eggs and buttermilk with electric mixer.
- Add dry mix to the buttermilk and eggs mixture. Mix.
- Add melted better to bowl and mix again.
- Make pancakes by pouring ⅓ cup at a time on hot griddle. Yields 12-13 pancakes.

MORE ABOUT ROGOTZKE'S FABULOUS SYRUP

Their award winning 100% pure maple syrup took First Place in the 2006 and 2009 Minnesota State Fair. They also won First Place in 2003 and Second Place in 2005. This fabulous syrup is available in a variety of sizes, just check out: www.simplegiftssyrupandsalmon.com You'll also find maple butter, which is 100% pure maple syrup boiled, chilled, then churned into a creamy consistency. It's fantastic on toast, muffins, pancakes, or whatever you can think of.

*"I have never had a bad meal here!
Some of the best breakfasts in town,
and a place I can go where I trust the
food to be delicious, organic, and local."*
-Nicole Bedard

RED FLANNEL HASH

Why stick to boring old hash browns when you can make this colorful combo of sweet potatoes, beets, carrots, and more?

INGREDIENTS:

10 cups diced sweet potatoes

2 cups diced beets

1 ¼ cups diced carrots

2 cups diced green pepper

1 cup diced onion

1 teaspoon white pepper

1 ½ teaspoon sea salt

1 ½ teaspoon thyme

½ cup olive oil

DIRECTIONS:

- Peel carrots and sweet potatoes. Dice all ingredients in 1-inch cubes.

- Boil beets until tender, then drain and peel.

- Toss all ingredients in large mixing bowl, spread on sheet pan and roast in oven at 450° for 25 minutes or until potatoes are tender. Yields about 10 cups.

Note:

After baking and slicing these can be wrapped individually and frozen.

CARAMEL – APPLE FRENCH TOAST

Start with French toast, then load it up with sweet apples, whipped cream, and caramel sauce. It's a seven-year old's version of heaven on earth.

INGREDIENTS:

1 ¾ pounds cinnamon rolls

6 slices Texas Toast

6 eggs

2 tablespoons cinnamon

¼ cup sugar

2 cups heavy cream

1 cup chopped pecans

1 ¼ cups diced apples (about 2 small)

DIRECTIONS:

- Cut cinnamon rolls and Texas Toast into 1" X 1" squares.

- Place into a large mixing bowl.

- In a separate mixing bowl mix eggs, cream, sugar, apples, pecans and cinnamon.

- Add the cinnamon rolls and bread to the liquid and mix until moist and binding.

- Grease 2 large loaf pans. Divide the mix into each pan and press down lightly.

- Bake at 350 degrees for 50 to 60 minutes. Prick the center to ensure it is fully cooked. Cool completely.

- Remove from pan and slice into 1 inch slices. Dip each slice into beaten eggs in a bowl and fry in a skillet as you would regular French Toast.

SCOTCH EGGS

Looking for a light, healthy alternative to salads? You may want to turn the page. Eggs coated with sausage and then fried are a favorite pub food, especially with mustard sauce. This dish is called the Mary and Jerry, after the customers who introduced Tom to the recipe.

INGREDIENTS:

6 hard-boiled eggs

1 pound Duluth Grill Breakfast sausage page 31, or use another favorite raw ground sausage

2 cups Panko Bread Crumbs

2 fresh eggs

1 cup all-purpose flour

DIRECTIONS:

* Set yourself up! In a small mixing bowl crack and mix two fresh eggs. Next, in another small mixing bowl place 2 cups of bread crumbs. Finally, in a third small mixing bowl place 1 cup of all-purpose flour.

* In a separate mixing bowl mash the breakfast sausage to make it pliable. Portion chunks into about 2.5-ounce balls (roughly a little larger than a golf ball).

* Take all six hard-boiled eggs and coat them in all purpose flour by rolling them around in the all-purpose flour bowl you created.

* Wrap each floured egg in the sausage that you have just portioned. Be sure to stretch the sausage all the way around the egg so it is completely covered.

* Next, roll the sausage wrapped egg in the freshly mixed eggs and cover in raw egg.

* Then immediately roll the egg in your bread crumbs to completely cover all surface area of the scotch egg. Repeat until all six eggs are breaded.

* Place each egg on a baking sheet and bake at 375 for about 20 minutes or until the internal temperature is at 165 degrees (great deep fried also!). Yields six eggs.

History of an Egg

While some dishes at the Duluth Grill are original creations, the Scotch Egg has a long and disputed history. London retailer Fortnum & Mason claims to have invented the dish in 1738 as travelling food for the wealthy. But Neil Chambers, the owner of the Handmade Scotch Egg Company, says they were a poor man's lunch made from leftovers. Either way, they're tasty. (Source: Adam Edwards of The Telegraph)

CORNED BEEF HASH

Erin go Bragh! Get a taste of the Emerald Isles on your breakfast plate with this hearty meal. "Corned" refers to the large grains of salt historically used to preserve the meat. Irish corned beef was a popular product in the 17th century as it provided a good, tasty protein source that kept well over long sea voyages. It eventually lost favor with much of the world but continued to be an important food source during the Second World War.

DIRECTIONS:

- Dice corned beef and potatoes into ¼ inch cubes.
- Heat 2 tablespoons oil in skillet.
- Add onions and cook until softened.
- Add corned beef and potatoes and cook until heated thoroughly.
- Mix in heavy cream and serve. Yields 4 servings.

INGREDIENTS:

1 pound (4 cups) cooked corned beef brisket

12 ounces (2 ½ cups) cooked potatoes

¾ cup diced onion

¼ cup heavy cream

2 tablespoons oil

BREAKFAST SAUSAGE

Breakfast sausage gets most of its flavor from sage, but the other spices are also important. Play around with the amount of crushed red pepper and syrup depending on if you like yours hotter or sweeter.

INGREDIENTS:

1 pound ground pork

2 ½ teaspoons sage

½ teaspoon salt

½ teaspoon black pepper

¼ teaspoon dry marjoram

¼ teaspoon dry oregano

½ teaspoon Smokey paprika

¼ teaspoon fennel seeds

½ teaspoon crushed red pepper

⅛ teaspoon cloves

⅛ teaspoon cinnamon

¼ cup cooked wild rice

2 ½ teaspoons maple syrup

¼ cup blueberries

3 tablespoons water

DIRECTIONS:

- Place all of the spices together and mix thoroughly.
- Add the 3 tablespoons water to the spices and stir until incorporated.
- Mix ground pork and spices together thoroughly.
- Portion into patties and fry until brown and cooked through. Yields 4 servings.

MEDITERRANEAN OMELET

Start your day with a little luxury. With basil, capers, and Kalamata olives, this is like Italy on a plate. Try serving with a simple caprese salad.

INGREDIENTS:
3 large organic eggs

4 – 6 basil leaves (chiffonade)

1 teaspoon capers - drained

8 kalamata olives - sliced

1 stalk fresh scallion

Approximately 10 roasted red pepper strips (⅜")

Approximately 10 diced tomato pieces (½" inch square)

2 tablespoons crumbled feta cheese

Tip:
To serve a bigger group, place the omelets on plates in your oven and set to 180° to hold and serve together.

DIRECTIONS:

- Heat a seven inch non-stick sauté pan over a medium heat. Get the pan very hot. While your pan is heating set up ingredients in a mixing bowl.

- In a separate mixing bowl, crack your eggs. Whip them up completely so there is no variation in color.

- Add the capers, olives, scallions, and roasted red peppers to the whipped eggs.

- Add enough oil to your sauté pan to coat the pan or you can use a non-stick spray.

- Pour the egg mix into the pan and roll the mix around the pan to cook it evenly. Flip the omelet once it becomes firm enough to slide around in a disc form.

- Once flipped, place ¾ of the tomatoes, feta cheese, and basil chiffonade in the omelet and the other ¼ aside to top the omelet.

- Pull the pan from the heat when the egg is completely cooked and gently slide the omelet onto a plate folding it in half on the plate. Top with the remaining ingredients and serve. Yields one omelet.

ROASTED RED PEPPER & PESTO OMELET

Feta provides a salty kick to this elegant, Italian-inflected breakfast. Make it a lunch by serving with a piece of baguette and a green salad.

INGREDIENTS:

3 large organic eggs

2 tablespoons pesto (page 9)

About ¼ cup roasted red pepper strips (8 strips)

3 ounces crumbled feta cheese

DIRECTIONS:

- Heat a seven inch non-stick sauté pan over a medium heat. Get the pan very hot to the touch. While your pan is heating set up ingredients in a mixing bowl.

- In a separate mixing bowl crack your eggs and add the pesto. Whip them up completely so there is a nice consistency to the mix.

- Add enough oil to your sauté pan to coat the pan or you can use a non stick spray.

- Pour the egg mix into the pan and roll the mix around the pan to cook it evenly. Flip the omelet once it becomes firm enough to slide around in a disc form.

- Add ¾ of your roasted red peppers and feta cheese in the center of the omelet.

- Pull the pan from the heat when the egg is completely cooked and gently slide the omelet onto a plate folding it in half on the plate. Top with the remaining ingredients and serve. It's nice to accent the omelet with some dollops of pesto on top. Yields one omelet.

D
U
L
U
T
H

G
R
I
L
L

TARRAGON PEPPER OMELET

A little tarragon goes a long way, but this unusual twist on an omelet has just the right amount. Get a little French in your morning! Feel free to substitute regular pesto.

INGREDIENTS:

3 large organic eggs

2 tablespoons Tarragon pesto

Approximately 15 roasted red pepper strips (⅜")

4 tablespoons crumbled feta cheese

DIRECTIONS:

- Heat a seven inch non-stick sauté pan over a medium heat. Get the pan very hot to the touch. While your pan is heating set up ingredients in a mixing bowl.

- In a separate mixing bowl crack your eggs and add the tarragon pesto. Whip them up completely so there is a nice consistency to the mix.

- Add enough oil to your sauté pan to coat the pan or you can use a non stick spray.

- Pour the egg mix into the pan and roll the mix around the pan to cook it evenly. Flip the omelet once it becomes firm enough to slide around in a disc form.

- Add ¾ of your roasted red peppers and feta cheese in the center of the omelet.

- Pull the pan from the heat when the egg is completely cooked and gently slide the omelet onto a plate folding it in half on the plate. Top with the remaining ingredients and serve. It's nice to accent the omelet with some dollops of pesto on top. Yields one omelet.

Tarragon Pesto

- *1/2 cup chopped fresh basil*
- *1/4 cup chopped fresh tarragon*
- *2 Tablespoons extra virgin olive oil*
- *Salt to taste*

Blend. (Add more or less olive oil to change the consistency).

GRIZZLY BARS

Pineapple and banana add distinctly tropical notes to this chewy dessert.

INGREDIENTS:

1 12-ounce can pineapple chunks, drained and food processed

6 ounces banana puree

2 egg whites

¼ cup honey

¾ teaspoon vanilla

2 cups whole wheat flour

¼ cup flax seeds

1 ½ teaspoons baking soda

1 ⅛ teaspoons salt

1 teaspoon cinnamon

½ teaspoon nutmeg

¼ teaspoon cloves

2 ¼ cups oatmeal

¾ cup raisins

½ cup dried cranberries

½ cup pecans

DIRECTIONS:

- Preheat oven to 350°

- Grind the flax seed in a food processor for 5-10 minutes until flax is broken down to half of its original size.

- In a large mixing bowl, add the dry ingredients and mix well.

- In a separate mixing bowl mix the wet ingredients well.

- Pour wet mix into the dry mix and stir until all is combined (do not over-mix).

- Grease a 9 x 13-inch cake pan.

- Add mix to cake pan, smooth out batter and place in oven.

- Bake for 30 minutes.

- Cut into squares and serve.

PUMPKIN SPICE CAKE

Pumpkin offers both starch and sweetness, so it's an ideal base for tasty gluten-free cakes. This can be enjoyed for breakfast or dessert.

INGREDIENTS:

⅓ cup plus 1 tablespoon vegetable oil

¼ cup honey

3 eggs

1 ¾ cup buckwheat flour

2 ½ cups powdered sugar

15 ounces pumpkin puree

2 teaspoons chia seeds

½ teaspoon sea salt

1 tablespoon cinnamon

1 tablespoon ginger

1 tablespoon cloves

1 teaspoon xanthan gum

½ cup hot water

1 ½ teaspoon baking soda

DIRECTIONS:

- Preheat oven to 350°

- In a mixer combine oil, honey, eggs, buckwheat, powdered sugar, chia seeds, salt, cinnamon, ginger, cloves and xanthan gum. Mix well.

- Separately add baking soda to hot water, dissolve and add to mix.

- Grease a 9 inch round cake pan and pour batter into pan.

- Bake at 350 degrees for 55-65 minutes or until a pick comes out clean.

- Cool in pan and then remove and cool on rack.

If the sky isn't actually grayer in Lincoln Park, it certainly feels that way. The Duluth Grill is just a block from the freeway, and if you stand in the parking lot, you can watch pickup trucks and beater cars spitting out clouds of exhaust while semis thunder by on the road. The cars must feel at home, since there are two gas stations on one block and the asphalt is basically everywhere. Many of the buildings are squat and brown, from the hardware store to the nonprofit down the street. The Holiday Gas Station and the Burger King share a parking lot, which flows into another lot shared by the Motel Six and the Duluth Grill. It's hard to imagine a worse place for a farm.

But when the phone company dug up the corner of the lot in 2009, Tom found himself with a big pile of dirt—and an opportunity. A customer told him that if the restaurant had had landscaping there, the phone company would have been obligated to restore the lot to its previous condition instead of leaving it a big mess. A landscaper said he would bring in 11 rocks with mulch for

Tom assesses the crops.

$3,700, but a customer who owned a field full of rocks soon made a better offer. Tom could have whatever he wanted, as long as he was willing to get it himself.

"I pulled out my own pickup truck out to her field," Tom says. "That summer we hauled eight hundred rocks back. Customers said, 'What are you doing?' and I said 'I'm building gardens.'"

That first year, he installed gardens that were 60 feet

GARDENS IN THE PARKING LOT

The gardens continue to expand

long and two feet wide on the side of the restaurant. He started with basic herbs, expanded into broccoli and cauliflower, and soon started supplying even more vegetables. When his staff ran into shortages late at night, no one had to wait for a Sysco truck. Everything they needed for a quick resupply was literally just out the back door.

"We had tomatoes, peppers, basil," Tom says. "We'd run out at night just from short ordering. No problem, they'd go out and harvest more."

But little gardens have a way of becoming big gardens, and the Duluth Grill's parking lot operation was no exception. The Duluth Timber Company gave Tom a good deal on recovered wood from Vlasic pickle brining tanks, so he built a 60' x 5' plot in 2010 and another 60' x 2' plot and 6 beds out

Farm manager François Medion gets a little help.

in front in 2011. François Medion came on board part time as a farm manager, then full time the next year. Now, the gardens grow chioggia beets, rat-tail radishes, ground cherries, sunflowers, castor bean plants, and more. Hanging flowerpots further beautify the entrance to the restaurant with primrose, milkweed, lilies, and sedums, along with horseradish and tulips.

These beautification projects are starting to impact the neighborhood. While the Duluth Grill's efforts to clean up the yard have got them plenty of press attention, they were intended mainly to enhance the property so it

wouldn't be looked at as a rundown part of town. But as the Duluth Grill started cleanup, others followed.

"With us doing this our neighbors are starting to do things," Tom says. "We cleaned our yard, and all of a sudden they had two kids out there for a week cleaning."

Some of it has been a team effort. During the second year, Matt Boo of Duluth Stove and Fireplace helped Tom take out a chain link fence that had separated their two properties. He stuccoed the posts for the gardens and the two put in railings. Now, the two neighbors both have better curb appeal—and better views from their own front windows.

"When you walk out in our yard, even in the winter, it feels like a yard instead of a big dirt parking lot," Tom says.

And even bigger projects are afoot. In 2012, the Duluth Grill placed squash and pumpkin plants on the roof. Watered primarily by rainwater and condensation from the air conditioners, they should provide hundreds of pounds worth of product. It's all a way to make the most of the land, no matter how many cars are parked on it.

"We're increasing the productivity with the same amount of property," Tom says. "We're developing more intense crop on the same amount of land just by working and thinking." **DG**

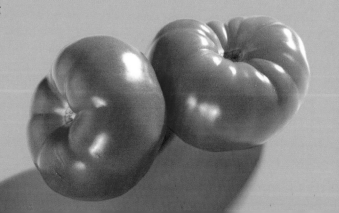

Soups & Stews

What's in a Name?

No one knows where the word "hobo", which came to prominence in California in the 1890s, comes from. Various people have suggested it comes from "hoe-boy", "ho! beau" and "homeward bound". We've arbitrarily decided it comes from Hoboken, New Jersey. Please don't ask us to defend that hypothesis.

HOBO SOUP

Whether or not you're an actual hobo (and if you are, thanks for buying our book), you'll find this soup hearty and filling. You can ad lib the vegetables and use whatever you like—this is an excellent late-summer way of using your garden's bounty (or a great opportunity to clean out your fridge). Plus, with plenty of meaty bison, and a tasty broth, it's a good way to get kids—or husbands—who might not normally like vegetables to give them a try.

INGREDIENTS:

2 quarts water

1 ¾ cups carrots

1 cup corn

1 cup onion, diced

1 cup celery, diced

1 ¼ cups green beans

¾ cup barley

1 28-ounce can diced tomatoes

1 ½ cups tomato juice

2 ½ teaspoons parsley flakes

¾ teaspoon black pepper

¾ teaspoon seasoned salt

1 ½ teaspoons granulated garlic

1 ⅔ tablespoons beef base

1 pound bison roast

DIRECTIONS:

- Cut bison roast into 1 inch chunks.
- In a large, heavy saucepan add all ingredients and bring to a boil.
- Reduce heat and simmer, stirring occasionally, for 1 ½ to 2 hours or until bison, veggies and barley are tender. Yields 4 quarts.

CHICKEN TORTILLA SOUP

This south-of-the-border inspired stew uses basic ingredients, so you won't have to get anything from the grocery store except a bit of fresh cilantro. ¡Olé!

INGREDIENTS:

¾ pound cooked chicken, diced

2 teaspoons mushroom base (some brands may not be gluten free or vegan)

1 cup corn

3 tablespoons roasted red peppers, diced

⅓ cup onion, diced

1 4-ounce can diced green chilies

2 tablespoons cilantro, chopped

1 teaspoon seasoned salt

1 teaspoon granulated garlic

1 ¾ teaspoon cumin

½ teaspoon white pepper

¼ teaspoon red pepper flakes

6- 6 inch corn tortillas

6 cups water

DIRECTIONS:

- Heat 1 tablespoon oil in a heavy pan.
- Add onions and sauté until soft.
- In a food processor grind 6 tortillas with 1 cup of water.
- Once they are pulverized to a mush add them to the 6 cups cold water and stir.
  - Add this to the onions in the pan and begin to cook.
    - Add all the rest of the ingredients into the pan.
      - Bring to a boil, reduce heat and simmer until thick and creamy. Yields 8 cups.

SMOKY SPLIT PEA SOUP

This hearty split pea soup is taken up a notch with chipotle peppers and paprika, which make it quite warming on a winter day.

INGREDIENTS:

1 quart split peas (dry)

2 cups diced onion

2 cups diced celery

4 cups diced sweet potatoes

3 minced cloves of garlic

2 – 29 oz. cans diced tomato with juice

2 dried chipotle peppers

1 teaspoon smoky paprika

½ teaspoon sea salt

1 ¼ gallons water

¼ cup vegetable soup base (some brands may not be gluten free or vegan)

DIRECTIONS:

Soak the dried chipotle peppers in boiling water to reconstitute. Puree them in a blender or food processor.

Simply add all the ingredients to a large soup kettle and bring to a boil. Reduce heat and simmer for one hour. Cook until beans soften to the bite.

WILD RICE CHICKEN OR TURKEY SOUP

Use up Thanksgiving leftovers in this tasty blend of wild rice, veggies, and stock.

INGREDIENTS:

2 cups cooked wild rice   8 cups water

3 tablespoons vegetable base
(some brands may not be gluten free)

¾ pound cooked chicken or turkey

1 cup celery, diced   1 cup carrots, sliced

½ cup cornstarch   2 cups heavy cream

¾ teaspoon sage   ½ teaspoon white pepper

½ teaspoon salt

DIRECTIONS:

In a mixing bowl mix cornstarch and heavy cream, set aside for later.

In a large, heavy pan add the rest of the ingredients, except wild rice, and bring to a boil. Add cornstarch mixture and mix well. Reduce heat to medium, add wild rice and simmer for 30 minutes, or until vegetables are tender, stirring occasionally. Yields 10 cups.

BLACK BEAN SOUP

Dried beans are cheaper than canned beans, and they take up less space. This soup is healthy, and if you omit the cilantro, it's also exceptionally budget-friendly.

INGREDIENTS:

1 pound black beans (soaked in 1 gallon water overnight)

2 cups diced onion

1 cup corn

1 cup diced green peppers

1 cup diced tomatoes with juice

half a jalapeño—diced small

1 minced garlic clove

1 small can green chilies

1 tablespoon cumin

¼ teaspoon cayenne pepper

1 teaspoon crushed red pepper

1 teaspoon granulated garlic

1 teaspoon onion powder

1 teaspoon seasoned salt

1 teaspoon sea salt

1 quart water

2 tablespoons vegetable base (some brands may not be gluten-free or vegan)

½ bunch cilantro (chopped)

Tip:

Cook this for at least two hours, as the flavor only gets better. The biggest mistake you can make is not cooking it long enough.

DIRECTIONS:

Puree half of the soaked beans in a food processor or blender. Add onions, green peppers, garlic, green chilies, and all the spices to a large kettle that you will prepare the soup in. With a little oil sauté for five minutes. Add the rest of the ingredients and the rest of the soaked beans. Bring to a boil.

Turn down heat and simmer for 2-3 hours stirring occasionally until beans breakdown and soup thickens.

FIRE ROASTED TOMATO STEW

While the Duluth Grill concentrates on comfort food, the fire-roasted tomato stew with lamb shanks was an unexpected hit.

INGREDIENTS:

2 tablespoons oil

2 medium onions, diced into ½ inch chunks

1 tablespoon minced garlic

½ tablespoon cumin

¼ teaspoon cinnamon

¼ teaspoon cardamom

¼ teaspoon cayenne pepper

¾ teaspoon marjoram

½ pound red potatoes, cut into ½ inch wedges

1 cup water

1 cup chickpeas, cooked

1 28-ounce can fire roasted tomatoes

½ pound carrots, cut in ½ inch diagonal slices

6 tablespoons cilantro, chopped

¼ cup whole garlic cloves, add to stew whole

2 tablespoons red curry paste (some brands may not be gluten-free or vegan)

DIRECTIONS:

- Heat 2 tablespoons oil in a large pot over medium heat.
- Add onions and cook until onions soften, stir often, cook for about 5 minutes.
- Add garlic, continue to stir and cook for about 1 minute.
- Add spices and cook until fragrant, about 1 minute.
- Add all of the rest of the ingredients; cover and cook on a low heat until all veggies are soft. Add more liquid as needed to prevent scorching. Yields 8 cups.

TOMATO BASIL SOUP

This creamy, home-style twist on tomato soup is perfect on its own or as a luxurious accompaniment for grilled cheese.

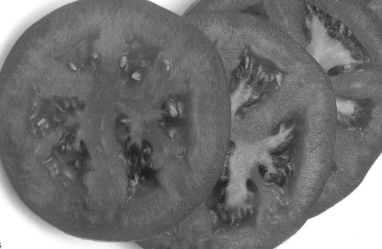

INGREDIENTS:

1 cup diced onion	14.5-ounce can diced tomatoes
3 ½ cups tomato juice	1 cup milk
¼ teaspoon salt	2 tablespoons salsa
¼ teaspoon white pepper	½ teaspoon sugar
1 cup heavy cream	¼ cup cornstarch
2 tablespoons fresh basil, chopped	

DIRECTIONS:

In a mixing bowl mix cornstarch and heavy cream. Set aside for later.

In a large, heavy saucepan add the rest of the ingredients and bring to a boil. Reduce heat, add the cornstarch mix. Stir well and simmer for 30 minutes on low. Yields 2 quarts.

LUMBERJACK BISON STEW

If you're the kind of rugged lumberjack who is too busy cutting down trees to keep Kitchen Bouquet in stock, you can leave it out.

INGREDIENTS:

1 pound bison pot roast cut into 1 inch cubes

2 tablespoons flour

⅓ teaspoon salt

⅓ teaspoon black pepper

1 tablespoon canola oil

1 tablespoon beef base

1 medium onion cut into 1 inch dice

1 cup celery, diced

1 bay leaf

2 to 3 cups water (depending on desired thickness of stew)

½ tablespoon Kitchen Bouquet

1 cup whole mushrooms

1 cup carrots cut into 1 inch dice

1 cup green beans

½ cup corn

2 tablespoons butter

4 tablespoons flour

DIRECTIONS:

- In a large, heavy saucepan heat oil; add beef, flour, salt and pepper and cook until browned.
- Add onions, celery, carrots and mushrooms.
- Cook until veggies are slightly tender.
- Add water, Kitchen Bouquet and bay leaf; stirring to loosen the browned bits from the pan.
- Simmer on medium heat for 30 minutes until veggies are tender.
- Add green beans and corn. Continue to cook until all veggies are tender.
- In a separate pan make the roux by melting 2 tablespoons butter and adding 4 tablespoons flour.
- Cook over low heat for 3 to 5 minutes.
- Mix roux into simmering stew to thicken.
  Yields 8 cups.

Tip:

You can an use leftover cooked bison from pot roast (page 94).

LAMB SHANKS

Searing these lamb shanks allows the all-important Maillard reaction to take place, browning the meat and creating important flavor compounds. Then, they're slow-baked with duck fat to dissolve connective tissue, which makes them meltingly tender.

INGREDIENTS:

Sear:

1 cup cici flour

¾ teaspoon dried marjoram

¾ teaspoon dried rosemary

¾ teaspoon salt

4 lamb shanks

oil as needed

Bake:

4 ounces duck fat (you may substitute salted butter)

2 large garlic cloves, minced

¾ tablespoon black pepper

SEAR DIRECTIONS:

- Mix the cici flour with all of the spices.
- Coat each shank in the flour.
- Add oil to a large heavy pan and sauté each shank to a caramelized, brown surface.

BAKE DIRECTIONS:

- Using a 6 inch deep pan stand the braised shanks in an upright position.
- Add in duck fat.
- Mix garlic and pepper together and sprinkle over the shanks.
- Cover and place in a 300 degree oven.
- Bake for 3 to 5 hours until the shanks are falling off the bone tender yet moist.
- Pour off the duck fat stock and set aside.
- Chill and remove the fat and save. Duck fat can be used several times if the quality is intact.

Crazy About Confit

In cooking, the old informs the new. This dish is a twist on a classic French preparation called confit, when a salt cured piece of meat (often duck) is poached in its own fat. Slowly poaching lamb in duck fat gives it a unique flavor boost and subtly hints at the old French traditions.

THURSDAY MORNING AT THE GRILL

It's eight o'clock in the morning on an unseasonably warm January day. There are already twenty people scattered around the dining room, sipping coffee or reading that day's copy of the Duluth News-Tribune. People come here to eat (veggie omelets, hash browns with homemade ketchup), but only a few of the tables still have plates—the morning has moved on to the conversation and coffee stage.

Waitresses in tie-dyed Duluth Grill shirts roam from table to table, pausing to smile, refill coffee, or drop off checks. The clink of plates and rattle of silverware from the kitchen mingle with the hiss of frying pans and the low murmur of conversation. There's a table of five heavyset state troopers in uniform and two squad cars parked just outside the window. At two tables near mine, old men with baseball caps and worn faces sit by themselves. One is holding the newspaper out a few feet away from his face, his arms stretched as if he were trying to look at a two-page photo spread all at once. The other is just staring into space, silent, his cup of coffee ahead of him. He sits like this for several minutes.

"I guess Carl was talking about selling his pickup," he says to the man with the newspaper. His voice is low and grumbly.

The man at the neighboring table lowers his paper and shares his thoughts on the matter. The two talk about Carl for a few minutes, then get up and leave.

A waitress hovers over another table, where two women have just arrived. She repeats the side dishes fluidly, with the practiced assurance of someone who does this fifty times a day.

"Toast? Pancakes? Cinnamon roll? Caramel roll? French toast?"

"Pumpkin spice bread," the customer says.

"OK!" The waitress smiles. That's on the menu too.

It's a good morning at the Duluth Grill. **DG**

SERVING AND BEING SERVED

The Duluth Grill is often praised for having good service, and Tom says that it all starts with having good workers. The most basic need of an employee is money, and the Duluth Grill attracts better people by offering more. While front of the house workers can rely on tips, Tom says the Grill is careful to make sure back of the house employees are taken care of as well.

"We pay anywhere from like 11 to 15 dollars an hour," Tom says. "Dishwashing would start at like 9. It's Duluth, it's a competitive wage."

In addition to higher wages, the Duluth Grill offers health insurance to anyone working 16 hours a week or more. Managers don't guarantee eyeglasses or dental, but do have their own methods for making those available. The Grill is a popular restaurant, and sometimes an eye doctor or dentist is willing to barter for gift cards.

"Bartering is kind of the oldest form of transactions," Tom says. "The baker wants something done they'll bring bread to the blacksmith, kind of along the lines of that."

A few years ago, the Grill started offering a cash bonus to all its back of house workers. As traffic keeps rising (the Duluth Grill has seen increases of 30% or more each year

Jaima puts the finishing touches on a slice of cheesecake.

Server Jill Knutson with her friend's baby Ezra.

for the last few years), front of house staff benefits from higher tips. Tom says that his employees have learned to put a premium on good service. Ultimately, it's the backbone of the business, a lesson he makes sure to emphasize.

"You know, the customer doesn't care that you haven't had a smoke break, or you're hungry, or you're having a conversation of what you did last night," Tom says. "Without customers coming into the building you won't get a paycheck and if you don't get a paycheck you probably wouldn't show up."

As a result, the servers are courteous and friendly, consistently knowledgeable and helpful. They're often singled out for praise on the comment cards the restaurant collects throughout the week or complimented on Internet rating sites like Yelp. In 2012, they even placed second in the city for Best Restaurant Service in *Duluth~Superior Magazine's* Best Of Awards. It all comes down to an attitude that puts the guest first.

"If I were to come into your house, what would you do?" Tom says. "You wouldn't stare at me blankly. You'd look at me and say, 'Hey, come in, would you like something to drink?' Make the customer feel like they're coming in and being treated like a guest." **DG**

THE PEOPLE BEHIND THE FOOD

KATHY JENSEN: TALMADGE FARMS

If you're going to buy pickles, you should buy local pickles. And if you're going to buy local pickles, you should buy them from Talmadge Farms. Tom says that owner Kathy Jensen is a get-things-done type who doesn't take nonsense from anyone.

"She's like this little lady but you can tell she works with her hands and her body," Tom says. "Her arms are muscular—if that's a nice way to say it for a lady—and she definitely knows what she's doing."

"Her arms are muscular—if that's a nice way to say it for a lady— and she definitely knows what she's doing."

Talmadge Farms is a fixture at farmer's markets and festivals around the area for jellies, jams, pickles and more. The Duluth Grill buys between 15 and 45 gallons of pickles a week, and also sells her jams. The Horseradish Jelly has a sweet but bold taste and pairs well with cream cheese and crackers, the Hot Pepper Jelly works as a steak sauce, and the Strawberry-

Rhubarb is a great match for breakfast foods. Jensen's farm has built a great reputation for quality over the years, and Jensen has got the processes down—even if she's been doing things for so long that she doesn't remember exactly why she does them that way.

"You talk to someone who's very established and you ask 'why did you do that step?'" Tom says. "They look at you and say 'I don't know—because that's how it works'."
DG

IKE STROHMAKER

Most farmers know their subjects well, but beekeeper Ike Strohmaker might know a little bit more than average. He sells between 1,500 to 2,000 pounds of honey each year to the Duluth Grill for use in smoothies, vegetable dishes, and more. And if you ask him about bees, Tom says, you can get quite an earful.

PHOTO BY TOM HANSON

Louis Hanson and Ike Strohmaker

"When we started off talking to him he says 'I don't know much about bees, but this is what I can tell you',"

"After two hours of talking about bees, I don't think he's quite done yet".

Tom says. "After two hours of talking about bees, I don't think he's quite done yet."

Tom describes Ike as a kind-hearted, passionate man with a well-used truck and a pair of overalls. He hails from the metropolis of Togo, Minnesota, which has less than 15 people per square mile. He sends holiday cards every year, asks how the Hanson family is doing, and will sit down and give them advice on beekeeping. Thanks to his help, the Duluth

Grill's beekeeping program keeps improving. It's all part of an ecosystem of local producers. There's a certain competitiveness between suppliers, but in the end everyone is dedicated to improving local agriculture.

"I guess it's weird being asked about the relationship," Tom says. "Because like I said, many times there are no words for it. You understand each other." **DG**

The Duluth Grill hives (pictured here) have benefitted from Ike's advice.

Starters

SALMON CAKES/ BURGERS

Nothing says "manly" like a burger, and nothing says "manly and trying to cut down on his cholesterol" like a salmon burger.

INGREDIENTS:

1 pound poached salmon

1 ¼ cups bread crumbs

2 green onions, sliced

½ cup mayonnaise

1 tablespoon lemon juice

½ teaspoon salt

½ teaspoon white pepper

1 teaspoon dill

2 eggs

oil

Note:

These are a great alternative to conventional burgers for those who won't eat meat. See page 76 for more ideas of toppings other than the delicious Cucumber–Dill sauce featured here.

DIRECTIONS:

- Flake salmon into ½ inch pieces.

- Add all other ingredients into a large mixing bowl and mix well.

- Add the salmon to the mixing bowl and gently mix together just enough to bind well but not to break up the salmon.

- Form into patties about 2 inches thick, or smaller if making salmon cakes.

- Heat oil in heavy skillet, add salmon patties and fry to a golden brown.

- Yields 5-6 larger cakes or several smaller cakes.

CUCUMBER–DILL SAUCE

This cooling sauce works well with fish, and tempers spicier entrees.

INGREDIENTS:

1 cup Greek yogurt

¼ cup, peeled, seeded and diced cucumber

¾ teaspoon dill

¼ teaspoon fresh garlic, minced

⅛ teaspoon salt

dash white pepper

DIRECTIONS:

In a mixing bowl mix all ingredients together until incorporated. Chill until serving. Yields 1 cup.

CURRIED POLENTA

Tasty, vegan and gluten-free, these wraps are a creative flavor combination and especially good with Roasted Red Pepper Vinaigrette (page 81).

LETTUCE WRAPS

INGREDIENTS:

3 cups Cici flour (garbanzo bean flour)

1 tablespoon mushroom base

1 teaspoon cayenne pepper

2 teaspoons curry powder

1 teaspoon turmeric

2 teaspoons granulated onion

1 teaspoon granulated garlic

5 cups water

four leaves Bibb lettuce

four slices of avocado

four large slices roasted red pepper

chopped cilantro to serve

vinaigrette to serve

DIRECTIONS:

- In a large saucepan mix all ingredients until incorporated.
- Bring to a boil over medium heat. Stir occasionally until polenta starts to heat up and thicken.
- Stir continuously as it begins to boil.
- Control the heat as you want this to cook for some time. The longer it cooks the more smooth the polenta will be.
- Once it is fully cooked pour the polenta out into a 10 x 15 x 1 inch pan.
- Let it cool in the pan for 10 to 15 minutes. Cut into cubes.
- To each piece of lettuce, add one piece of avocado, one piece of roasted red pepper, and a few cubes of curried polenta. Sprinkle with chopped cilantro and vinaigrette.

Tip:

Because of their brilliant color and small, convenient size, these make perfect pass-around appetizers. They're the perfect way to convince dedicated meat-eaters that veganism isn't all bad, and they also make a good case for gluten-free eating.

BUFFALO TOFU STRIPS

Chicken wings—why bother? Everyone knows the point is the hot sauce, crunchy coating, and blue cheese dressing. So, you might as well replace the chicken with tofu. Just make sure to eat these quickly, as the texture can suffer if they sit a long time.

INGREDIENTS:

1 12-ounce extra firm block of tofu
(cut into ¼ inch strips)

1 cup cornstarch

1 cup vegetable oil

1 6-ounce bottle of Louisiana hot sauce or to taste

DIRECTIONS:

- Place cornstarch in a covered container. Place half the tofu in cornstarch and toss thoroughly.

- Heat oil to 350 degrees in a deep saucepan.

- Carefully place strips in oil. Fry until crisp, flipping if necessary. Pull from oil and place on a paper towel.

- Repeat with other half of tofu strips. Toss in hot sauce and serve immediately.
  Yields 3 ½ cups.

Talking Tofu

If you're new to the world of tofu, it can be a little confusing. There are several varieties of tofu, from silken tofu sold in Tetra Paks to extra firm tofu sold wrapped in plastic. You want the firmest tofu you can get for this recipe. Before cooking, there are two ways to make it even firmer. One technique is to pop the slices in the freezer, then thaw and squeeze out any remaining water before using. Another way is to slice it, wrap it in a paper towel, and weigh it down with a heavy pot or a book for around an hour. Try both and see which appeals to you most.

CHIPS THREE WAYS

GUACAMOLE

Don't be scared of it because it's green. This creamy spread is perfect with chips or as part of a Mexican meal.

INGREDIENTS:

6 avocados

¼ cup red onion

1 tablespoon minced garlic

1 teaspoon cayenne pepper

¼ cup lime juice (about 1 lime)

½ cup cilantro

1 teaspoon cumin

½ teaspoon salt

DIRECTIONS:

- Remove the pit and skin from the avocados. Mash in a mixing bowl and set aside for later.
- Combine onion and the rest of the ingredients in a food processor, puree until smooth.
- Stir the mixture from the processor into the mashed avocados.
- Refrigerate until ready to use. Yields about 2 cups.

SALSA

Salsa is Spanish for "sauce", but it's most commonly used for this familiar spicy concoction. If you don't have Pico de Gallo, you can substitute two roma tomatoes, one bell pepper, half a red onion, salt, pepper, cumin, lime juice, and a quarter cup of chopped cilantro. Or just buy the Pico de Gallo.

INGREDIENTS:

1 cup diced tomatoes

½ cup tomato juice

½ tablespoon minced garlic

¼ cup lime juice

1 tablespoon olive oil

½ teaspoon black pepper

½ teaspoon salt

½ teaspoon granulated garlic

⅛ teaspoon cayenne pepper

¼ bunch cilantro

1 cup Pico de Gallo

DIRECTIONS:

In a food processor add tomatoes, tomato juice, cilantro garlic, lime juice, olive oil and all spices. Pulse until you get a chunky blended salsa mix. In a mixing bowl add salsa mix and Pico; mix by hand. Refrigerate until use. Yields about 2 ½ cups.

GREEN SALSA

Salsa verde is a fun alternative to the more common red salsa.

INGREDIENTS:

2 pounds tomatillos

8 ounces poblano peppers

1–2 jalapeno peppers

1 habanero pepper

¼ cup cilantro, chopped

1 tomato, diced and seeded

¼ cup red onion, diced

1 green pepper, diced

1 4-ounce can green chilies

salt and pepper to taste

DIRECTIONS:

- Preheat oven to 450 degrees.

- Cut poblanos and jalapenos in half. Take off stems but leave seeds in.

- Place on baking sheet along with the tomatillos and roast for 20-30 minutes (skins should be blackened).

- In a food processor blend the tomatillos, peppers and cilantro.

- Pour into a large bowl and mix well to incorporate all ingredients.

- Stir in tomato, red onion, green pepper and green chilies. Add salt and pepper to taste. Mix well. Makes about 5 cups.

Note:

When you are handling hot peppers, you should always wear gloves!

STIRATO

This is a large rustic loaf with an airy and springy crumb perfect for bruschetta, hearty French toasts or simply to enjoy with a meal. We like to make this loaf hefty at about 3 pounds when finished, to get the perfect ratio of crumb to crust and to be able to cut big slices. The unique sourdough-like flavor and texture comes from refrigerating the dough—thereby "retarding" it—for up to 24 hours.

INGREDIENTS:

3 and 1/2 cups all purpose flour (1 lb)

3 and 1/2 cups high gluten flour (1 lb)

Or alternatively 7 cups bread flour (2 lb)

2 teaspoons dry active yeast (0.3 oz)

1 tablespoon salt (1 oz)

3 cups warm water (about 85° F)

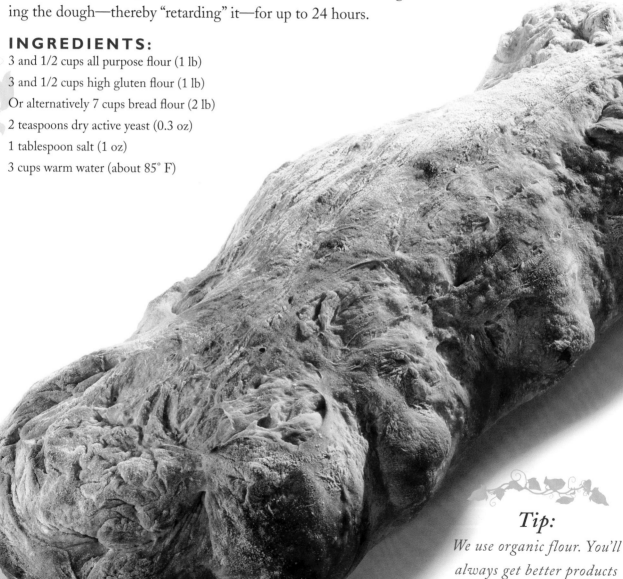

Tip:
We use organic flour. You'll always get better products with organic flour.

DIRECTIONS:

Mixing & Kneading

In a large bowl, mix all the dry ingredients first then add the water and knead rapidly with one hand while holding the bowl with your other hand. Use a rotating motion while kneading, lifting the dough off the sides of the bowl until water and flour are totally incorporated. You should end up with relatively wet and very tacky dough (the wetness will make for airy bread and light crumb). Let the dough rest for 20 minutes then knead it three to five minutes, dusting with flour as necessary for easy handling.

First Rise (the "Retardation" Period)

Place the dough in an oiled container with a lid and large enough to allow the dough to double in size. Alternatively you can use an oiled bowl and cover the dough with plastic wrap. Let the dough sit at room temperature for about 45 minutes, until you can see that the fermentation has began then place in the refrigerator for 12 and up to 24 hours.

Second Rise

When done with the "retardation" period, on a floured surface, shape the dough into a tight ball and place it on a tray with waxed paper brushed with oil. Place the tray inside a plastic bag and lightly spray the inside with warm water, it is very important during this second fermentation to not let the dough dry and form a crust which would hinder a full development. Place in a warm area away from drafts.

Depending on the ambient temperature, it will take from one to two hours for the dough to warm up, for the yeast to awaken and to complete the fermentation. Your dough will be ready to shape and bake when doubled in size showing signs of bubbles under the skin and still springing back when poked with a finger. In winter, if your home is cool, a good place to do the final proofing is inside your oven that you have warmed on the lowest setting and turned off.

Tip:

Can't find high gluten flour?
Substitute 2 lbs. bread flour
for both kinds of flour.

Baking the Bread

Pre-heat your oven to 550° F. Generously sprinkle the dough ball with flour and place it on a floured surface. The shaping must be done rapidly but without over-manipulating the dough and loosing the gas trapped inside. Squeeze the ball to give it an oblong shape then grip each end and, while lifting, stretch it (Stirato) while giving it a waving motion (it helps the stretching). Stretch-it so it fills the length of the tray you'll be baking on. Place the shaped loaf upside-down (this prevents having all the bubbles on the top of your bread and gives it a beautiful rustic look) on a baking tray lined with waxed paper. Place immediately in the oven, and do this quickly: you want to lose as little heat as possible. You can spray water in the oven or throw ice cubes on a pan in the bottom of the oven to help your bread get a good "oven spring". Turn the oven temperature down to 475° and bake 20 to 25 minutes until golden-brown.

Cool on a rack.

FOCCACIA (or *Fougasse*)

The Foccacia is visually arresting and a full flavored bread ideal for dinner parties or to enjoy on its own. It freezes very well to be used at a later date, makes great toasts for canapés or appetizers and can be turned into sumptuous croutons for summer salads. Perhaps what we love the most about this bread is its versatility, your imagination and preferences are the limits, just like a pizza, the flavoring and topping ingredients are all for you to play with. For this bread too, we use the "retardation technique" for enhanced flavor and texture.

The flavors of Italy shine through here, with basil, rosemary, and olive oil taking center stage. It should go without saying that the quality of your olive oil will make a difference.

INGREDIENTS:

3 cups all purpose flour (12 oz)

1 and 1/4 cup high-gluten flour (4.8 oz)

[Or alternatively, 4 and 1/4 cups of bread flour (16.8 oz)]

1 teaspoon dry active yeast (0.1 oz)

2 teaspoons salt (0.4 oz)

1 and 3/4 cup warm water (85-90° F)

1/4 cup extra-virgin olive oil (we like full flavored oil for this) plus extra for brushing on top of bread

2 tablespoons of fresh or dried herbs of your choice

Garnishes according to your taste

DIRECTIONS:

Mixing & Kneading

Follow the exact same procedure as for the Stirato (previous pages) in the mixing, kneading, "retardation" and final proofing.

Incorporate the herbs with your dry ingredients and the olive oil with the water. Again you should end up with relatively wet dough very soft and pliable which will turn into soft and airy bread.

Generously sprinkle the dough ball with flour and place it on a floured surface. The shaping must be done rapidly but without over-manipulating the dough and loosing the gas trapped inside. Gently press the dough ball down with your fingers, forming a disk. Grab opposite sides of that circle and pull in every direction until your dough is about 12-15 inches wide. If you make this bread regularly, you might want to practice stretching it like pizza dough by using your knuckles and spinning it, it is a lot gentler on the dough.

Baking

Pre-heat your oven at 500° F. If your oven goes higher you can bake at a higher temperature, like a pizza this bread can take a lot of heat and is better for it but you better keep a close eye on it, your chances of burning it increases exponentially.

Place your formed loaf on a baking tray lined with waxed paper. Now garnish your bread and brush it generously with olive oil. At this point, if you wish to have a loaf without large bubbles and more even in shape, you can poke the dough by pressing your stretched fingers making dimples every couple inches.

Bake for about 20 minutes. Creating steam isn't necessary for this bread. Cool on a rack.

Flavoring

Rosemary and roasted pepper foccacia: add 2 tablespoons of chopped fresh rosemary to your dry ingredients. After your loaf is shaped and resting on the baking tray but before you brush it with oil, apply 5 pointy slices from a roasted sweet red pepper pressing gently to make them adhere to the dough and forming an irregular 5 points star. Brush generously with olive oil. Finish with a sprinkling of shredded mozzarella.

Roasted garlic and sun-dried tomato foccacia: Roast a dozen or so garlic cloves and let them cool down. Chop 2 or 3 sun-dried tomato wedges. After you mixed your dough and gave it its rest stretch it as much as you can without breaking it then stud it evenly with the cloves and tomato bits. Roll it so as to incorporate all the ingredients. Proceed with the refrigeration, proofing and shaping. Once shaped, brush it generously with olive oil and sprinkle with grated parmesan. Bake.

Tip:

For best results, invest in a kitchen scale. Professional bakers measure by weight, not by volume.

FALAFEL

Like chickpeas but prefer your food fried? Hearty, filling, and vegan, crunchy falafel is like State Fair food from the medieval Middle East.

INGREDIENTS:

2 cups soaked, raw garbanzo beans

1 tablespoons minced garlic

1 teaspoons cumin

½ teaspoon turmeric

½ teaspoon salt

¼ cup diced onion

2 tablespoons chopped cilantro

2 tablespoons water

½ tablespoon lemon juice

⅛ teaspoon cayenne pepper

2 ½ tablespoons cici flour (chickpea flour)

DIRECTIONS:

- Place dried chickpeas in a bowl, covering with cold water. Allow to soak overnight.

- Place onion, cilantro and garlic on the bottom of a food processor or blender and the beans on top. Process until the batter is smooth.

- Add the flour and baking powder and process until thoroughly combined.

- Scoop batter into balls (about the size of a golf ball) and flatten slightly, or flatten into a patty if you are going to serve as a burger.

- Fry in 2 inches of oil on medium until golden brown (5-7 minutes). Yields 10 falafel.

MOROCCAN HUMMUS

Hummus is the Rolling Stones of food products —hundreds of years old but still hip. It's got healthy fat from olive oil and good vegetarian protein from chickpeas.

INGREDIENTS:

2 cups cooked garbanzo beans

1 tablespoon honey

4 tablespoons lemon juice

⅛ bunch of cilantro

1 tablespoon cumin

1 tablespoon minced garlic

¼ teaspoon salt

½ teaspoon cayenne pepper

½ cup olive oil

DIRECTIONS:

- Combine all ingredients in a food processor or blender.

- Place cilantro, garlic and spices on bottom to ensure an even blending of ingredients.

- Process until smooth. Label, date, refrigerate. Yields about 2 cups.

Four out of five chickens say they like the Duluth Grill. The omelet section of the menu might raise a few eyebrows (if chickens had eyebrows), but the fact that all the eggs are both organic and cage-free means that the animals are treated like kings (if chickens had kings). Unlike battery-raised chickens, who sometimes have to live out their entire lives in a space smaller than a sheet of paper, these lucky birds get to amble around the yard and live out their little chicken lives to the fullest. Kirk Bratrud, general manager of the Chester Creek Café, is another big fan of organic, cage-free. Like the Duluth Grill, the Chester Creek Café uses only organic, cage-free eggs. For both restaurants, it ultimately comes down to a concern for the birds.

"These are chickens that still have beaks," Kirk says. "They are actually able to go out into a field and exercise and do what chickens do, then come back in to roost and they produce their eggs."

While the decision to go organic, cage-free seemed like the right thing to do, Louis Hanson says it wasn't an easy one to make. Eggs are a classic high-margin item, since they're much cheaper than most proteins but can cost nearly as much on a menu. Cage free eggs can cost 20 to 30 cents more per egg than battery eggs, so in order to preserve some of the margin it's necessary to raise prices.

The Hansons briefly considered offering organic, cage-free alongside regular eggs. But forcing cooks to keep track of who wanted *light* brown eggs and who wanted *medium* brown eggs, on a busy Saturday morning, with fourteen orders coming in at the same time? Not a bad plan, if you

CHICKEN TESTED.
CHICKEN APPROVED.

like having your office stormed by a mob of angry employees with frying pans. As it was they decided to just take the plunge and charge more.

"We thought if we slow down a little bit I guess we'll be okay," Louis says. "As soon as we did that we got busier. That was kind of our moment of saying people are starting to recognize what food actually is, and care about the food that they're putting into their bodies. That's our cage-free organic egg and how we started evolving our menu again."

That early change drove a lot of other changes as well. Now, the turkeys in the turkey dinner are free-range, the beef is grass-fed, and the salmon is wild caught. The menu at the Duluth Grill is largely focused on higher quality food, which is more expensive, but, thanks to market trends, just as profitable.

"If you look at Whole Foods Co-op, for example, their business is increasing every year," Louis says. "People are seeking that really good quality food." **DG**

"These lucky birds get to amble around the yard and live out their little chicken lives to the fullest."

Sides

GARLIC PARSNIPS

Potatoes: they're not the only root vegetable anymore. Parsnips taste like mild turnips, and they're loaded with fiber and potassium.

INGREDIENTS:

5 fresh parsnips

¼ cup olive oil

1 whole bulb smashed garlic cloves

1 teaspoon salt

½ teaspoon white pepper

3 sprigs fresh rosemary

DIRECTIONS:

- Fill a medium sauce pan half full with water and bring to a boil.

- Pre-heat oven to 325 degrees.

- Meanwhile, peel and wash parsnips. Cut in half and then quarter lengthwise so they are ½ inch strips.

- Smash garlic with the blade of the knife so the garlic breaks apart.

- Place parsnips in boiling water for 5-8 minutes or until al dente, or you can poke them with a fork but they are still firm.

- Drain parsnips thoroughly.

- Toss parsnips, oil, salt, pepper and garlic cloves and place on a sheet pan lined with aluminum foil.

- Roast in oven for 15 minutes or until garlic turns golden brown.

- Meanwhile, pull rosemary off of the sprig and roughly chop.

- After you pull parsnips and garlic out of the oven, toss with chopped rosemary and white pepper until completely coated.

COLESLAW

Creamy, crunchy coleslaw gets an exotic twist from a hint of cardamom.

DRESSING INGREDIENTS:

1 cup mayo

2 tablespoon sugar

½ tablespoon apple cider vinegar

¼ teaspoon white pepper

¼ teaspoon salt

¼ teaspoon cardamom

¼ cup red wine vinegar

MIX INGREDIENTS:

1 large head of diced cabbage. Want more color? Mix green and red cabbage.

1 cup or 5 ounces craisins

4 tablespoons red wine vinegar

DIRECTIONS:

- Add dressing ingredients to food processor or blender and mix until fully incorporated.
- Dice cabbage and place in large bowl.
- Pour 4 tablespoons red wine vinegar over cabbage and toss.
- Pour dressing over cabbage and toss until fully incorporated. Yields about 12 cups.

SESAME GREEN BEANS

This Asian-inspired side dish gets added crunch from sesame seeds.

INGREDIENTS:

1 pound (4 cups) green beans

1 tablespoon sesame oil

½ teaspoon rice vinegar

Salt and pepper to taste

¼ teaspoon white sesame seeds
¼ teaspoon black sesame seeds

DIRECTIONS:

Bring 2 quarts of water to a rolling boil. Add salt to water. Clean and trim the beans and blanch in the boiling water for about one minute.

Dry the beans thoroughly and place in mixing bowl and toss with ingredients. Refrigerate. Yields 4 cups.

CREAMY CORN POLENTA

Polenta on its own can be rather boring, but when you load it up with butter and heavy cream you'll have a delightful substitute for mashed potatoes.

INGREDIENTS:

1 cup heavy whipping cream

5 cups water

¼ cup grated Parmesan cheese

2 cups corn meal

1 teaspoon sea salt

4 tablespoons butter

DIRECTIONS:

- Place all ingredients into a large saucepan.
- Bring to a boil stirring constantly.
- Pour hot polenta into a greased 9 x 13 inch cake pan.
- Bake at 350 degrees for about 30 minutes.
- Cut into 4 x 3 inch cubes.

SQUASH WITH

APPLES AND WALNUTS

I f you're not a vegan, you can replace the oil with butter for an even richer version of this warming winter dish.

INGREDIENTS:

2 pounds squash (cut into 1 inch cubes)

½ pound green apples (diced into ¼ inch cubes)

¾ cup chopped walnuts

3 tablespoons oil (or melted butter)

½ teaspoon cinnamon

¼ teaspoon nutmeg

¼ teaspoon salt

⅛ teaspoon white pepper

3 tablespoons brown sugar

DIRECTIONS:

- Preheat oven to 450.

- Place the squash, apples and walnuts in a bowl and coat with melted butter.

- In a separate bowl mix cinnamon, nutmeg salt and pepper.

- Pour spices over the squash mix and mix together thoroughly.

- Place all ingredients on a sheet tray.

- Sprinkle brown sugar evenly on top and bake for 20 minutes or until squash is just fork tender. Serves 4-6.

SWEET POTATO SIDE

Sweet potatoes contain vitamins B6, C, and D, along with potassium, iron, and carotenoids. Plus—let's be honest with ourselves—they're delicious.

INGREDIENTS:

2-3 medium-sized sweet potatoes

Cooking oil

Brown sugar (for topping)

Sea salt (for topping)

Powdered sugar (for topping)

DIRECTIONS:

- Chop sweet potatoes in half the long way. Next, make ½ inch cuts across the short way.

- Lay all pieces flat on a cookie sheet and bake until soft. (About 30 minutes).

- Next, in a large skillet heat the cooking oil. Drop the sweet potatoes in the hot oil and fry both sides until golden brown.

- Serve topped with sea salt, brown sugar, and powdered sugar.

  Yields four side servings.

BRUSSELS SPROUTS

It's time to get rid of preconceptions. You can transform your opinion of Brussels Sprouts simply by roasting them instead of boiling them. This is one of the Duluth Grill's most-asked-for recipes.

INGREDIENTS:

1 pound Brussels sprouts
(trimmed and cleaned)

3 tablespoons honey

1 ½ tablespoons olive oil

DIRECTIONS:

* Cut sprouts in half and tear off outer leaf set.
* Toss all ingredients in a bowl and place on a sheet pan.
* Bake in the oven at 350 degrees for 30 minutes with the blower off.
* Turn blower on and bake for another 5-10 minutes. Serves 4-6.

STUFFING WITH PORK SAUSAGE

This hearty stuffing is a great side dish, but works as a filling lunch when paired with a simple salad.

INGREDIENTS:

1 pound ground pork

1 cup onion, diced

1 cup celery, diced

½ cup dried cranberries

6 cups water

½ pound butter

2 tablespoons chicken base

½ tablespoon thyme

½ tablespoon sage

½ tablespoon white pepper

1 teaspoon salt

1 ½ pound croutons

2 eggs

DIRECTIONS:

- In a large sauté pan brown ground pork.
- Add onions, celery, and cranberries and cook until onions are translucent and pan is deglazed.
- In a separate pot boil water, butter, chicken base and all of the seasonings.
- Once boiling add sausage mix from the sauté pan to the boiling water.
- Place croutons in a large mixing bowl. Pour the boiling mixture over the croutons and stir together. Add the eggs and continue to mix.
- Once mixed place all contents into a greased roasting pan and bake for 1 hour or until the top is golden brown. Yields 16 cups.

CARROTS WITH MAPLE GLAZE

Maple syrup brings out the natural sweetness in carrots. This fall-inspired side dish is a good way to use up extra garden produce.

INGREDIENTS:

1 pound fresh carrots (washed and cut into ½ inch slices)

1 ½ tablespoons melted butter

¾ tablespoon maple syrup

salt

white pepper

DIRECTIONS:

- Place carrots in a saucepan and cover with water.
- Bring water to a boil and cook carrots for 3-4 minutes or until al-dente (soft firm to the tooth).
- Remove from heat and drain thoroughly.
- Cover with melted butter, syrup and salt and white pepper to taste.
- Place on sheet pan and roast in oven at 350 degrees for 30 minutes until lightly caramelized. Serves 4-6.

WILD RICE ORZO PASTA SALAD

Why stick to boring old regular pasta when you can dress it up with wild rice? Bring a taste of Minnesota to your next gathering with this creative side.

INGREDIENTS:

½ cup dry orzo pasta (cook before making)

4 cups pre-cooked wild rice

¾ cup diced green peppers

3 tablespoons diced red peppers

¼ cup diced red onion

¾ cup diced broccoli

2 tablespoons fresh basil (chiffon ode)

¾ teaspoon oregano

½ salt

½ teaspoon white pepper

2 tablespoons chopped fresh parsley

¾ cup craisins

2 tablespoons balsamic vinegar

DIRECTIONS:

Combine ingredients in large mixing bowl and refrigerate. Yields about 6 cups.

WILD RICE SIDE DISH

Parsley and craisins brighten up nutty wild rice, and the cheese gives it a hint of creaminess.

INGREDIENTS:

½ cup wild rice (about 2 cups cooked)

¼ cup craisins

¼ cup shredded cheese

1 tablespoon parsley, chopped

¼ teaspoon white pepper

¼ teaspoon salt

DIRECTIONS:

Cook wild rice according to directions. Mix all ingredients together and serve warm. Yields 4 servings.

CRANBERRY SAUCE

This couldn't-be-simpler cranberry sauce gets a subtle additional sweetness from apple juice.

INGREDIENTS:

4 cups cranberries

1 cup sugar

⅓ cup apple juice

DIRECTIONS:

Combine all ingredients in a large saucepan and cook, whisking regularly, until all of the cranberries break down and create a thick sauce.
Let cool. Refrigerate. Yields about 2 cups.

MAKE YOUR OWN BURGER

D U L U T H   G R I L L

Burgers 5 Ways
1. *Salmon Burgers (pg 53)*
2. *Falafel Burgers (pg 64)*
3. *Hand-pattied 100% organic, grass-fed bison*
4. *Hand-pattied 100% organic grass-fed beef*
5. *Wild Rice Burgers (facing page)*

Bison Burger

Beef Burger

Roasted Red Pepper Vinaigrette, pg 81

Roasted Garlic Cloves, pg 79

Cranberry Mayonnaise, pg 81

BBQ Sauce, pg 79

Tartar Sauce, pg 93

Mustard, pg 78

WILD RICE BURGER

Wild rice is a very healthy grain and makes a substantial base for a vegetarian burger or melt.

INGREDIENTS:

Seasonings:
1 teaspoon white pepper
1 teaspoon salt
1 ½ teaspoons granulated garlic
4 teaspoons cumin
1 ½ teaspoons crushed red pepper

Base:
1 cup Panko (Japanese bread crumbs)
1 ½ cups mayo
4 eggs
1 cup diced mushrooms
5 cups cooked wild rice

DIRECTIONS:

- Add seasonings to base ingredients and mix well.

- Using a metal 1-cup measuring cup scoop up rice mixture and form into a patties about 2 inches thick.

- In a pre-heated heavy skillet heat 2 tablespoons oil and add patties.

- Pan fry until heated through and nicely browned on both sides. Yields 6 servings.

Salmon Burger

Wild Rice Burger

Cucumber-Dill Sauce, pg 53

Spicy Thai Peanut Sauce, pg 80

Ketchup, pg 78

Caramelized Onions, pg 80

Balsamic Reduction

KETCHUP

One of the most controversial recipes in the history of the Duluth Grill, the homemade ketchup is something people love or hate. It's a bit sweeter than Heinz, with a little more texture and a subtle hint of spice.

On the other hand, Tom says that Heinz himself wouldn't enjoy what his ketchup has become.

"If Heinz came alive today he would not be proud of that recipe," Tom says. "He'd go, 'how did these ingredients get into my recipe?'"

INGREDIENTS:

2 tablespoons olive oil

¼ cup diced onion (about half of a medium onion)

1 teaspoon minced garlic (about one clove)

29-ounce can of tomato sauce or use equivalent fresh tomatoes

¼ cup honey	1 tablespoon molasses
⅛ cup cider vinegar	⅛ cup red wine vinegar
dash cayenne pepper	dash cinnamon

1 tablespoon corn starch added to a bit of cold water to make slurry

DIRECTIONS:

* Add olive oil to a medium sauce pan and turn heat to high. Saute onions until they turn translucent. Add garlic and sauté until garlic begins to change color. Do not burn.

* Add the rest of the ingredients except the corn starch slurry. Whisk together very thoroughly. Bring to a boil and turn heat to low and simmer for one hour.

* After 1 hour pour ketchup into a blender and blend until smooth.

* Strain sauce through a strainer back into the sauce pan. Add corn starch slurry and return to a boil. You can add a little more corn starch if you would like a thicker ketchup or leave out if you like it more thin.

* Label, date, refrigerate. Yields about 3 cups.

MUSTARD

Mustard is often hailed as the King of Condiments. Okay, that's not exactly true, but it is an excellent way to add flavor without adding calories.

INGREDIENTS:

2 tablespoons yellow mustard seeds

2 tablespoons black mustard seeds

⅓ cup boiling water

½ cup cider vinegar

½ tablespoon dry mustard

2 tablespoons honey

½ teaspoon onion powder

¼ teaspoon garlic powder

¼ teaspoon cinnamon

¼ teaspoon ground cloves

¼ teaspoons turmeric

DIRECTIONS:

* Combine all ingredients except water in a 1 quart container and store overnight

* Transfer mix to the food processor or a blender and blend until smooth.

* Add water to desired consistency and pour into a container to store. Yields about 1 cup of mustard.

Ketchup

Mustard

BBQ SAUCE

Liquid smoke and coffee bring this sweet-sour BBQ sauce down to earth.

INGREDIENTS:

½ teaspoon onion powder

2 teaspoons granulated garlic

2 cups ketchup

1 cup coffee

7 tablespoons brown sugar, packed

¼ cup cider vinegar

2 teaspoons lemon juice

2 teaspoons Kitchen Bouquet

2 teaspoons molasses

2 teaspoons Liquid Smoke

DIRECTIONS:

Mix all ingredients together in a heavy saucepan. Bring to a boil, reduce heat and simmer for 1 hour on very low heat. Yields 2 cups.

BBQ Sauce

ROASTED GARLIC CLOVES

Roasting garlic cloves under low, slow heat transforms them entirely. Instead of the pungent raw garlic flavors, you'll get a buttery, impossibly mild topping that's easy to spread and delicious on a burger with Gouda cheese.

INGREDIENTS:

30 peeled garlic cloves (about two bulbs)

2 tablespoons olive oil

DIRECTIONS:

* Pre heat oven to 350 degrees.

* In a bowl, toss garlic and oil.

* Line a baking sheet with aluminum foil.

* Place on a baking sheet and roast in an oven for 5 minutes.

* Remove from the oven and stir the cloves.

* Roast cloves for an additional 5 minutes or until the garlic is soft and easily spreadable. Yields 6 five-clove servings.

CARAMELIZED ONIONS

Caramelized onions make an elegant topping for pizza, pasta, or brats, and they're so easy to make.

INGREDIENTS:

2 cups onion

1 teaspoon balsamic vinegar

½ teaspoon olive oil

¼ teaspoon sugar

DIRECTIONS:

- Add all ingredients to a heavy saucepan and stir to combine.
- Cover and cook over medium-low heat, stirring occasionally, until onions are very soft. About 15-20 minutes
- Increase heat to medium and cook until onions turn brown but not burnt.
- Use as a topping for burgers.

SPICY THAI PEANUT SAUCE

Bring a touch of the Far East to your dinner table with this spicy peanut-forward sauce. It goes well with any meat dish, and it also makes a good topping for pasta.

INGREDIENTS:

½ cup chopped peanuts

⅓ cup sesame oil

¼ cup coconut milk

¼ tablespoon cider vinegar

1 clove of garlic

¼ tablespoon fresh ginger root

½ tablespoon molasses

¾ tablespoon balsamic vinegar

½ tablespoon kitchen bouquet

¼ tablespoon cayenne pepper

1 thai chili

½ teaspoon sea salt

2 tablespoons water

¼ tablespoon sriracha

¼ tablespoon honey

DIRECTIONS:

Place all ingredients in a food processor or blender. Mix until all ingredients are smooth and creamy. Label, date and refrigerate. Yields about one cup.

ROASTED RED PEPPERS

Like pickles or capers, roasted red peppers are high on taste but low on calories. Load as many as you like in pasta dishes or on sandwiches. And this couldn't-be-simpler method makes the process a snap.

INGREDIENTS:
4-5 fresh red peppers

Ice water in a large bowl

DIRECTIONS:
- Take all peppers and remove the seeds and stems.
- With tongs hold each pepper over an open flame until the skin of the pepper becomes wrinkled and dark in most areas (you can place peppers in the ice water bowl after roasting).
- Let peppers sit in the ice bath for about two minutes.
- Pull off the skin of each pepper. You now have roasted red peppers. Yields 4-5 peppers.

CRANBERRY MAYONNAISE

Mayonnaise is a versatile base, and it's often used in dips and sauces. Adding cranberries gives it a distinct but not overwhelming fruitiness.

INGREDIENTS:
¾ cup mayo

¼ cup cranberry sauce

DIRECTIONS:
Blend ingredients in a food processor or blender until smooth. Label, date, refrigerate. Yields 1 cup.

ROASTED RED PEPPER VINAIGRETTE

A zesty, creamy dressing with a hint of spice.

INGREDIENTS:
½ cup roasted red pepper

⅓ cup olive oil

⅛ cup red wine vinegar

2 tablespoons mayonnaise

1 ¼ tablespoons grated Parmesan cheese

1 tablespoon minced garlic

½ teaspoon ground basil

¼ teaspoon ground chipotle pepper

DIRECTIONS:
- In a food processor blend peppers, vinegar, garlic, basil and ground chipotle pepper until smooth.
- Add mayo and Parmesan and blend for 30 seconds.
- Keeping the processor running slowly add the oil (this should take about a minute or two just to add the oil).
- Pour into a jar and refrigerate until ready to use. Yields about 1 cup.

THE PEOPLE BEHIND THE FOOD

DICK MARTIN: LAKE SUPERIOR FISH

"If I could describe, like, a sailor guy who comes in…" Tom begins. "Not as extreme as the sailors you see on *Jaws* or anything wearing the floppy hat."

Fishing on the big lake takes its toll. There are intense weather conditions, odd hours, and just the general psychological effects that come with spending hours on a lake looking for fish. Tom describes Dick as a hard-charging type who knows how to get things done.

"He's got that nice aroma of fish when he comes in".

"You can tell he works hard and plays hard," Tom says. "He's got that nice aroma of fish when he comes in." Dick supplies whitefish and herring for the Duluth Grill's Friday night fish fries. As with other suppliers, Tom says it's important to respect the prices as they stand and not try to put the squeeze on.

"We understand that what the farmer tells us the price is, is the price," Tom says. "Much like us they have a budget. To haggle or negotiate a price down on someone just isn't right." **DG**

Big Hearty Entrees

TEMPEH BURRITO MIX

Tempeh is a nutty, chewy meat substitute especially popular in Indonesia. Here, it stars in a tasty, healthy burrito filling.

INGREDIENTS:

2 tablespoons oil

4 ounces tempeh (Diced into ½ inch cubes) (some brands may not be gluten-free)

2 tablespoons diced onion

1 4-ounce can diced green chilies

1 tablespoon minced garlic

½ tablespoon cider vinegar

½ tablespoon cumin

¾ teaspoon oregano

¼ teaspoon salt

¼ teaspoon black pepper

⅓ cup fresh salsa

1 15-ounce can black beans, drained and rinsed

1 15-ounce can Northern beans (with juice)

DIRECTIONS:

- In a large skillet heat oil.
- Add tempeh and onions and cook about 1 minute.
- Add rest of the ingredients, except beans.
- Cook about 5 minutes stirring frequently.
- Stir in beans and cook until heated thoroughly.
- Serve with warmed flour tortillas topped with sour cream, shredded cheese, salsa, guacamole and lettuce. Yields 4-6 servings.

CHIPOTLE PEPPER SAUCE

How do you say "zesty" in Spanish? Alongside the always-delicious blend of olive oil, onion, and garlic, a surprising combination of ketchup and coffee makes this sauce stand out.

INGREDIENTS:

1 cup diced onion

2 tablespoons minced garlic

2 tablespoons olive oil

1 small can chipotle peppers (pureed)

1 cup ketchup (some brands may not be gluten-free)

1 cup coffee

¼ cup brown sugar

¼ cup cider vinegar

¼ cup lemon juice

DIRECTIONS:

In large sauté pan add onion, garlic and olive oil. Sautee for 3 minutes. Add the rest of the ingredients and simmer for 20 minutes on very low heat. Remove from heat and allow sauce to cool.

ROASTED RED PEPPER SOUP

The bright taste of orange juice lightens up the smokiness of the roasted red peppers in this unusual soup.

INGREDIENTS:

2 cups diced onion (about 2 medium onions)

1 ½ tablespoons minced garlic (about 5 cloves)

¼ cup olive oil

32 ounces diced roasted red peppers

28 ounces stewed tomatoes

3 oranges (zest and juice)

¼ cup vegetable base to ½ gallon water

½ teaspoon black pepper

DIRECTIONS:

- In a medium stock pot, sweat onions and garlic with the olive oil on low heat until tender (sweating is much like sautéing only on low heat instead of medium to high heat).

- Add tomatoes to the pot and cook for 5 minutes.

- Dice roasted red peppers and add to the soup.

- Add water, vegetable base and black pepper. Simmer for 25 minutes.

- Zest oranges and then juice them. Add the juice and zest to the soup at the very end. Yields about 7 two cup servings.

Capsicum annuum:

The red pepper is a healthy choice. It's got tons of Dietary Fiber, Vitamin A, Vitamin C, Vitamin E (Alpha Tocopherol), Vitamin B6 and Folate, along with Vitamin K, Thiamin, Riboflavin, Niacin, Potassium and Manganese.

LASAGNA

Jaima Hanson's recipe was one of the earliest specials at the Duluth Grill. She says it brings back fond memories of her early home life. "My mom, she's Italian," Jaima says. "For birthdays we always got to pick what meal we wanted for our birthday and it was always lasagna. She never had a recipe—it's just like you throw things in, you taste. You just have to know it, so mine was different than hers. I thought, can I just make something for the restaurant? Lasagna came in first, and then it stuck."

INGREDIENTS:

Sauce:

1 28-ounce can crushed tomatoes

1 15-ounce can tomato sauce

1 15-ounce can diced tomatoes

½ pound Italian sausage links, diced

½ pound ground beef

3 tablespoons onion, diced

1 teaspoon garlic, minced

½ teaspoon granulated garlic

1 teaspoon basil

1 teaspoon oregano

½ teaspoon crushed red pepper flakes

1 teaspoon parsley flakes

salt to taste

white pepper to taste

2 teaspoons sugar

3 tablespoons grated Parmesan cheese

Cheese Filling:

15 ounces Ricotta cheese

16 ounces cottage cheese

1 egg yolk

salt and black pepper to taste

Other Ingredients:

½ pound (10) lasagna noodles cooked per directions on box.

36 pepperoni slices

14 ounces mozzarella cheese, shredded

1 cup Parmesan cheese, grated

DIRECTIONS:

- In a large, heavy pan brown the ground beef, sausage, onion and garlic. Drain.
- Cook 5 more minutes.
- Add the rest of the ingredients and heat slowly.
- Simmer for 2 hours stirring frequently.
- When sauce is done put a light layer of sauce on the bottom of a 9 x 13 inch baking dish.
- Lay 5 lasagna noodles on bottom of pan, overlapping slightly.
- Spread half of the cheese filling on top of the noodles.
- Spread half of the meat sauce on top of the cheese filling.
- Layer half of the pepperoni over the meat sauce.
- Sprinkle half of the Parmesan and half of the mozzarella over the pepperoni.
- Repeat all layers.
- Bake in oven at 350° for 30 to 45 minutes until the cheese is golden brown.

Tip:

In the middle use more sauce and less cheese, and on top use more cheese and less sauce. Otherwise you just get noodles pressed together.

VEGGIE LASAGNA

Why should meatheads have all the fun? Since lasagna is fundamentally about the pasta, there's no reason you have to load it up with meat to make it taste good. This version takes advantage of fresh vegetables, plenty of tofu, and walnut marinara.

INGREDIENTS:

Sauce:

1 cup diced onion about one medium onion

1 cup diced carrots about three medium carrots

1 cup sliced mushrooms

2 tablespoons minced garlic

⅛ cup olive oil

1 cup coarsely chopped walnuts

28-ounce can crushed tomato

28-ounce can diced tomato

28-ounce can tomato sauce

½ teaspoon white pepper

½ tablespoon granulated garlic

1 tablespoon basil powder

½ tablespoon dry basil leaves

1 tablespoon oregano

½ teaspoon salt

½ tablespoon crushed red pepper

1 tablespoon parsley flakes

½ cup grated Parmesan cheese

⅛ cup sugar

Tofu Filling:

24 ounce tofu

½ teaspoon salt

½ teaspoon black pepper

Lasagna Filling:

2 cups spinach

8-10 leaves fresh basil (chiffonade)

14-ounce can sliced black olives drained

4 ounces shredded Parmesan cheese

16 ounces shredded mozzarella (4 cups)

Noodles:

8-ounce box of gluten free or regular lasagna noodles.

DIRECTIONS:

Sauce:

* In a medium sauce pan, drizzle oil and sauté onion, garlic, carrots and mushrooms until onions are translucent.

* Add the rest of the ingredients, heat on medium heat, bring to a boil. Reduce heat and simmer for one hour, stirring frequently.

Noodles:

* Bring a large pot of water to a boil. Cook lasagna noodles according to directions on the box (about 10 minutes) until al dente.

* Drain noodles and toss in a little bit of olive oil to avoid sticking.

Lasagna filling:

* Mix all ingredients in a bowl.

Tofu filling:

* Put all ingredients in a blender or food processor and blend until smooth.

Assembling the lasagna:

* Spray a 9 by 13 pan with cooking spray.

* Spread a light layer of sauce (about two 8-ounce ladles) covering bottom of pan.

* Spread tofu filling on three lasagna noodles (about three heaping tablespoons on each noodle).

* Add one layer of lasagna filling (about 3 cups).

* Repeat for a total of three layers.

* Cover with foil and bake in oven at 350 degrees for 60 minutes.

* Remove foil and rotate lasagna in oven, bake for an additional 10 minutes or until internal temperature reaches 165 degrees.

* Remove from oven and let stand for 10 minutes before serving. Yields 12 servings.

TOFU & WALNUT MARINARA

Tofu gets a bad rap, but you might find this tasty sauce changes your mind. Use it wherever you'd use red sauce.

INGREDIENTS:

¼ cup diced onion

¾ teaspoon minced garlic

½ cup diced carrot

½ cup sliced mushrooms

1 tablespoon olive oil

1 28-ounce can crushed tomatoes

1 28-ounce can diced tomatoes

¼ teaspoon white pepper

¾ teaspoon granulated garlic

¾ teaspoon ground basil

¾ teaspoon oregano

¼ teaspoon salt

1 ¾ teaspoon crushed red pepper

1 ½ teaspoon parsley flakes

1 pack tofu

1 tablespoon sugar

¾ cups fresh spinach

1 ½ tablespoons fresh basil (chiffon ode)

¼ cup chopped walnuts

DIRECTIONS:

Sauté onion, garlic, carrots and mushrooms in olive oil. Add the rest of the ingredients; reduce heat and simmer for 1 hour, stirring frequently. Yields about 8 cups.

WHITEFISH DINNER

BAKED WHITEFISH

With just five ingredients, this preparation couldn't be simpler. If you're in a rush or don't like tarragon, replace the tarragon butter with regular butter.

INGREDIENTS:

6 whitefish fillets (8-10 ounces each)

Sprinkle lemon pepper

Sprinkle seasoned salt

1 lemon cut into 6 wedges

6 teaspoons tarragon butter

DIRECTIONS:

- Pre-heat oven to 350 degrees.
- Line a baking sheet with aluminum foil and brush with a thin layer of tarragon butter.
- Sprinkle both sides of fish with lemon pepper and seasoned salt.
- Place seasoned fish fillets on baking sheet and bake for 15 to 20 minutes or until internal temperature reaches 145 degrees and the fish is flaky. Yields 6.

LEMON AIOLI

A creamy fish sauce that works along the same principles as tartar sauce.

INGREDIENTS:

1 cup mayonnaise

1 teaspoon minced garlic

1 teaspoon Dijon mustard
(some brands may not be gluten free)

¼ teaspoon sea salt

A pinch of black pepper

Zest of 1 lemon

Juice of ½ a lemon

DIRECTIONS:

Blend all ingredients in a food processor or hand whisk in a mixing bowl.

Tip:

For super-easy juicing, cut an x in the uncut side of half a lemon and put in the microwave for 20 seconds. The juice will come right out when you squeeze it.

TARRAGON BUTTER

Tarragon is also known as dragon's-wort or silky wormwood, but this French herb offers more than just entertaining nicknames. With a fragrance similar to anise, it's the star seasoning in Béarnaise sauce and a great flavor in egg, chicken, or fish dishes.

INGREDIENTS:

8 tablespoons butter, room temperature

½ teaspoon lemon juice

¼ teaspoon minced garlic

salt to taste

white pepper to taste

1 tablespoon chopped fresh tarragon

DIRECTIONS:

Place all ingredients in a bowl and mix until fully incorporated.

Use on fish. This freezes well.

TARTAR SAUCE

Cilantro and lime juice brighten up an otherwise-classic tartar sauce.

INGREDIENTS:

1 cup mayonnaise

¼ cup sweet pickles, diced

½ tablespoon cilantro

½ teaspoon lime juice

¼ teaspoon honey

DIRECTIONS:

Add all ingredients to a bowl and mix thoroughly to a smooth sauce. Yields about 1 cup.

Tip:
For easier juicing, roll the lime around first before cutting it in half.

BISON POT ROAST

The Duluth Grill originally sold an easy-to-cook pot roast out of a bag, but Tom wanted them to make their own. Louis argued, asking why they should change something people already loved.

"And then he began to tell me, 'You know what, Lou? If the Food Network calls, and they want to showcase our pot roast, what are we going to tell them—that we're slicing open this bag and putting it in the warm au jus? Or are we going to say, we take this giant center roast from a bison, rub it in our own sauce, and cook it for five to seven hours?'

"I said, 'Well, if you want to do it, whatever.' Two years later, he called me up and said, 'The Food Network called. They want to feature our Dakota pot roast.' So he won."

INGREDIENTS:

1 Bison roast (about 4 pounds)

1 ½ tablespoons black pepper

1 ½ tablespoons granulated garlic

1 teaspoon celery seed

½ tablespoon salt

¼ cup minced garlic

1 ½ cups diced celery

1 ½ cups sliced carrots

1 onion sliced

4 cups water

DIRECTIONS:

- Line the bottom of a roasting pan with celery, onions and carrots.

- Place roast on top of vegetables.

- Make 4-5 cuts into the roast with a knife.

- Combine all dry ingredients with garlic and rub the top of the roast.

- Add water until roast is half submerged.

- Cover the pan with foil and cook at 300 degrees for 4-5 hours or until very tender.

- Slice roast and serve.

Note:

You can serve the cooked vegetables with the roast or save and use with leftover roast to make Hobo Soup.

CHICKEN MARSALA

Chicken marsala is simple but elegant, so it's a favorite on Duluth Grill catering menus. Make this ahead of time for your next potluck, Super Bowl party, or big family gathering and let the chafing dish (or crock pot) work its magic.

INGREDIENTS:

half quart (2 cups) sliced mushrooms

2 tablespoons Marsala wine

1 tablespoon cream sherry

1 cup heavy cream

¾ teaspoon oregano

¼ teaspoon white pepper

¼ teaspoon salt

1 tablespoon corn starch

Garbanzo bean flour

¾ teaspoon oregano

Olive oil for sautéing mushrooms and braising chicken

3 chicken breasts cut in half

DIRECTIONS:

* Sauté mushrooms on high heat in olive oil for a couple of minutes.
* Add marsala, sherry and cream to pan.
* Stir in and add seasonings—oregano, pepper and salt.
* Bring to a simmer. Mix remaining cream, some water, and cornstarch and add to sauce.
* While making sauce, coat chicken in flour and oregano mix and braise in olive oil. Yields 6 portions of chicken.

"WE'RE NOT GOING TO SERVE ANYTHING THAT ISN'T FOOD"

"**R**eading the diet syrup label we realized most of the ingredients in there were not pronounceable," Tom says. "Zero calories don't add up to clean food. I had a lady ask me 'Why did you take the diet syrup away?' I said 'We just made a decision that we're not going to serve anything that isn't food.'"

After several people requested a sugar-free syrup, they decided to invent their own. The new syrup is made from blueberries, water, stevia, cinnamon and salt, and chia seeds give it a surprisingly viscous mouth feel. It costs significantly more than the old sugar-free syrup, but Tom says it's worth it.

"I don't think we're doing this to make more money," Tom says. "I think we're doing this to build a bigger base that believes in our food."

RATATOUILLE

Tom enjoyed eating this at another local restaurant, but found it often wasn't done right—sometimes the Kalamata olives would be missing, another time it was the polenta. So he started making it himself. Like a cooked version of a big garden salad, ratatouille is a good way to use up extra vegetables.

INGREDIENTS:

3 large tomatoes

1 ½ large julienne cut onions

1 tablespoon pureed garlic

2 large diced bell peppers

28 ounces stewed tomatoes

3 diced zucchini

1 tablespoon dry oregano

1 diced egg plant

1 tablespoon dry basil

sea salt

½ tablespoon red pepper flakes

1 cup Kalamata olives

20 fresh basil (chiffonade) leaves

1 cup olive oil

¼ bunch fresh chopped parsley leaves

DIRECTIONS:

- Preheat oven to 325 degrees.

- Bring 2 quarts of water to a boil. Take each tomato, core and cut an "x" in the bottom cutting just through the skin. Place all 3 tomatoes in the boiling water for about one minute. Take out and set aside.

- Roast onions and bell peppers together first. Then roast eggplant and zucchini together.

- Cut onions into quarters and then julienne cut (thin strips). Toss in about 1 tablespoon of olive oil and some salt. Place on a sheet pan lined with aluminum foil and place in oven. Roast until onions begin to turn brown.

- Dice bell peppers, toss in about 1 tablespoon of olive oil and some salt. Place on a sheet pan lined with aluminum foil and place in oven. Roast until edges begin to turn brown.

- Dice the eggplant into one inch cubes including skin. Toss in about 3 tablespoons of olive oil and some salt. Place on a sheet pan lined with aluminum foil. Roast in oven until eggplant is soft and it begins to stick to the pan.

- Dice the zucchini into ½ inch cubes including skin. Toss in about 2 tablespoons of olive oil and some salt. Place on a sheet pan lined with aluminum foil. Roast in oven until zucchini begins to shrink and edges begin to turn brown.

- While vegetables are roasting, place ½ cup olive oil in a deep kettle. Turn heat to medium and start sautéing garlic. Peel the skin off tomatoes and place in kettle. Add canned tomatoes, oregano, dry basil and red pepper flakes and simmer with a cover partially over the kettle.

- Add roasted vegetables to the tomato sauce as they come out of the oven.

- Once all vegetables are added, chiffonade basil leaves and chop parsley leaves and add to tomato sauce.

- Add Kalamata olives to the stew and simmer for half an hour uncovered. Label, date, refrigerate any leftovers. Yields about 8 servings.

Tip:

Usually shortcuts are no problem, but this is one recipe you need to follow exactly. The vegetables and their cooking times have all been staged to work together.

SLOPPY JOE SAUCE & SLOPPY JOE FILLING

Childhood comfort food at its finest.

INGREDIENTS:

Sauce:

2 cups ketchup pulp or canned tomato sauce

¾ cup ketchup

½ cup diced onion

½ cup diced green pepper

½ tablespoon chopped garlic

2 tablespoons Dijon mustard

2 tablespoons honey

¼ teaspoon black pepper

olive oil

Filling:

3 cups water

1 tablespoon veggie base

2 cups TVP (Texturized Vegetable Protein)

½ tablespoon kitchen bouquet

DIRECTIONS:

Sauce:

- Add a little olive oil to a large sauce pan with high heat. Add onions, peppers and garlic. Cook until tender and onions are translucent.

- Add the rest of the ingredients for the sauce and cook for 30 minutes on medium heat.

Filling:

- Add water, veggie base, TVP and kitchen bouquet to a sauce pan and cook until TVP is tender and has a meaty texure.

- Add cooked TVP to sauce pan and cook for one hour on a simmer. Yields 8 servings.

MEATLOAF – GLUTEN FREE

A new spin on your grandma's classic, this meatloaf uses wild rice and buckwheat flour instead of bread crumbs.

INGREDIENTS:

2 pounds ground beef

¾ cup onion, diced

⅓ cup diced tomatoes (drained and pressed)

1 (4-ounce can) diced green chilies (drained and pressed)

3 tablespoons minced garlic

¾ cup cooked wild rice

1 ⅔ tablespoons buckwheat flour

2 eggs

1 teaspoons sea salt

1 ¼ teaspoons black pepper

¾ teaspoon granulated garlic

¾ teaspoon smoked hot paprika

2 ½ teaspoons onion powder

1 ½ tablespoons ketchup (set aside for later) (some brands may not be gluten free)

DIRECTIONS:

- Preheat oven to 350 degrees.

- Place all ingredients, except ketchup, into a large bowl and mix well.

- Place meatloaf into baking pan making sure to pack it tightly.

- Bake at 350 degrees for 1 to 1 ½ hours or until the internal temperature is 160 degrees.

- Smear ketchup over the top and cook an additional 5 minutes. Serves 4-6.

MUSHROOM GRAVY

Using mushrooms as a base makes this
vegetarian gravy rich and savory.
Who needs meat anyway?

INGREDIENTS:

Roux:

½ pound butter

1 cup flour

Base:

1 ½ quarts water

2 tablespoons mushroom base

¼ teaspoon granulated garlic

¼ teaspoon
white pepper

¼ teaspoon
onion powder

2 tablespoon
parsley flakes

1 cup diced onions

4 cups sliced mushrooms

¼ cup olive oil

DIRECTIONS:

Roux:

Bring butter to a slow boil on low heat, add
flour; stir constantly. Roux should not be
too thick. If too thin add more flour. Should
be the consistency of wet sand.

Base:

In large pot add water, mushroom base
and seasonings; bring to a boil. Add
roux, while stirring until gravy thickens.
Sauté onion and mushroom with olive oil.
Add to gravy.

PASTIES

Pasties (pronounced with a short "a" like "past", and don't you forget it) are usually associated with Cornwall in England. They date back to at least the 1300s, and as a favorite food among miners, they soon became popular on the Iron Range. Stuffed with meat, potatoes, and rutabagas, these are big and filling.

INGREDIENTS:

Crust:

8-½ cups flour

3 cups shortening

1-½ tablespoons salt

3 eggs

2-¾ tablespoons white vinegar

1 cup ice cold water

Filling:

3 medium peeled and cubed potatoes

2 medium diced carrots

½ medium cubed rutabaga

1 medium chopped onion

2 tablespoons minced garlic (about 2 cloves)

½ teaspoon seasoned salt

½ teaspoon salt

½ teaspoon black pepper

1 pound raw hamburger

1 pound raw mild Italian sausage

DIRECTIONS:

Crust:

- In a large mixing bowl, add the flour and salt and mix well. Add shortening to the flour and mix until flour has been absorbed by the shortening, leaving small marble sized chunks of shortening. Don't over mix.

- In a separate bowl, mix the eggs, vinegar and water. Mix well. Add the wet mix to the dry mix. Divide into 12 balls and roll out each one on a floured surface.

- Prepare the pasty mix ahead of time and refrigerate until dough is rolled out and ready.

Filling:

- In a large bowl, combine meat, potatoes, onion, rutabaga and chopped carrots. Season with salt, pepper and seasoned salt. Divide into 12 portions.

- Egg wash 12 pasty crusts. Place an equal amount of filling in the center of each crust.

- Fold crust over. Use a fork to seal the edges together.

- Again, egg wash each pasty top.

- Bake in an oven at 350 degrees for 60 minutes or until internal temperature reaches 165 degrees. Yields 12 pasties.

Pasties are such a popular item we make dozens at a time.

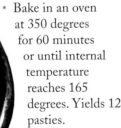

POACHED SALMON

ince it doesn't require oil or butter, poaching is one of the healthiest ways to cook. It works particularly well with a hearty fish like salmon, which has plenty of flavor on its own.

INGREDIENTS:

1 pound fresh salmon (peeled)

1 tablespoon celery

¼ teaspoon dill weed

1 small bay leaf

¼ lemon sliced

½ tablespoon chicken base (some brands may not be gluten-free)

¼ teaspoon celery salt

water

DIRECTIONS:

Add all ingredients, except salmon, to a large pot, bring to a boil. Add salmon and boil for 5 minutes. Remove salmon from pan and drain.

GINGER GLAZE

With only five ingredients, this glaze is simple but powerful. If you're vegan, char-grilled tofu has a strong enough flavor to hold up to it.

INGREDIENTS:

½ cup maple syrup

¼ teaspoon sea salt

¾ teaspoon Smokey paprika

½ tablespoon pickled ginger

¼ cup orange juice

DIRECTIONS:

Mix all ingredients in a food processor until incorporated. Transfer to a saucepan and cook down over low heat for 30 minutes until thickened. Use as a glaze on salmon. Yields ½ cup.

MUSHROOM PIE

This hearty, blast-from-the past vegetarian dish works well as the focal point of a meal.

INGREDIENTS:

Two 9-inch pie crusts

5 cups onion (julienne)

½ cup olive oil

4 quarts sliced mushrooms

1 pound cream cheese

2 teaspoons thyme

1 tablespoon black pepper

1 teaspoon salt

DIRECTIONS:

- In a stock pot sauté onions.
- Add mushrooms, cook for a few minutes, until mushrooms are tender.
- Cut cream cheese into cubes and add to the pot.
- Turn down heat to medium and stir until the cheese is melted.
- Add seasonings, stir until incorporated.
- Remove from heat.
- Serve in a pre-baked pie crust.

  Makes enough filling for 2 9-inch pies.

LOADED MAC & CHEESE

A thick, hearty, childhood favorite that will have the kids lining up for more.

INGREDIENTS:

3 lbs of precooked penne noodles

3 cups of our homemade cheese sauce

1 cup sautéed mushrooms

1 cup sliced roasted red peppers

8-10 strips of your favorite bacon chopped in ½ " pieces

1 cup of cheddar cheese

DIRECTIONS:

- Cook the penne pasta to al dente doneness.

- Place the pasta, sautéed mushrooms, peppers, and bacon together and toss.

- Add warm cheese sauce to the mix. Place in a casserole dish and top with shredded cheddar cheese. Place in the oven for 20-30 minutes until bubbling hot (165 degrees). Yields 6-8 servings.

CHEESE SAUCE

There's nothing like a good cheese sauce. Blending various types of cheese allows you to harmonize different flavor elements like nutty Gouda and mildly sweet Havarti. Use this for Mac and Cheese, pour it over a baked potato, or mix with salsa for a good chip dip.

INGREDIENTS:

1 Pint heavy cream

6 oz. shredded cheddar cheese

4 oz. shredded Havarti cheese

3 oz. Gouda cheese

¼ teaspoon white pepper

¼ teaspoon sea salt

DIRECTIONS:

- Pull your cheese from the cooler and let stand to room temperature (about an hour).
- Heat heavy cream in a double boiler or carefully in a sauce pan on medium high heat so not to scorch the cream.
- Bring to a boil and remove from heat.
- With a whisk stir in the cheese, salt and pepper until sauce is smooth and creamy.
- Add to pasta or store it in a covered container in the refrigerator.

GOING GREEN

As the Duluth Grill evolved, it has become increasingly environmentally friendly. Making homemade food has eliminated single-serving packages, which accumulate quickly in a high-volume restaurant environment.

"With half and half creamer cups and the little jelly packets and the ketchup bottles, we're into millions of packages." Tom says. "We'd use 5000 ketchup bottles a year."

The people of the Duluth Grill make their own chocolate sauce, caramel sauce, mustard, and salad dressings, along with ketchup, jam, and peanut butter. The upshot is thousands of dollars saved, along with millions of packages that don't need to be thrown away. Sour cream buckets and yogurt buckets are even re-used to plant seedlings at the Duluth Grill's urban farm.

But there have been other environmental changes as well. They switched to locally roasted Alakef coffee, which is Rainforest Alliance Certified Organic and fair-trade. Their decaf is made with the Rainforest Alliance mountain water process, an alternative to conventional decaffeination methods that use chemicals.

They also print their own menus on 100% post-consumer recycled paper, recycle all the paper, plastic, and cans they can, and light up the dining room with LED bulbs to save on electricity. In addition, they've cut dumpster usage by two thirds by pre and post composting food waste.

The Duluth Grill has also figured out some less obvious ways to protect the environment. Cooks used to reheat soups using the open flame of natural gas stove, a process that took 15-30 minutes ten times a day. They purchased more 2-quart containers and began using the microwave instead, then later switched to a steam boiler. Now, they heat up less product, use less energy, and keep the soup fresher by only heating what's needed.

In the winter, the Duluth Grill used to use harsh, aggressive sidewalk salt to keep roads and sidewalks safe. Since the restaurant is on a hill only two miles from Lake Superior, the environmental impact was significant. By mixing sidewalk salt with sand, they were able to go from using ten bags a year to just three bags.

There are also new projects in the works. The rooftop gardens should reduce cooling costs in the summer, and farm manager François Medion is hoping to feed the fish in the restaurant's fish farm with vegetable matter from the kitchen. It's all a way of giving back to the land for the sake of future generations. Conveniently, it often saves money as well. **DG**

> *"With half and half creamer cups and the little jelly packets and the ketchup bottles, we're into millions of packages." Tom says. "We'd use 5000 ketchup bottles a year."*

JOHN FISHER-MERRITT

John Fisher-Merritt is a spry man with gray hair who was living the green lifestyle before it was trendy. Tom describes him as an innovative guy with a strong back-to-nature vibe. But more than that, he's a farmer's farmer.

"He carries in 40, 50 pound boxes of potatoes without asking for any help," Tom says. "Looks like he does it a lot."

Tom had heard through the grapevine that Fisher-Merritt wasn't a fan of restaurants. They tended to ask for a lot by way of fresh produce but not want to pay very much for the privilege. But the Duluth Grill began to buy more and more from him. Now, their order includes carrots, tomatoes, cabbage, rutabaga, parsnips, garlic, red potatoes, and beets. They've developed a good working relationship.

"He's actually re-engineering his fields to fill our needs," Tom says. "You look at that-that's a lot of trust on both ends. It's kind of the [reverse] Walmart effect. We don't want to hurt him." **DG**

"He's actually re-engineering his fields to fill our needs."

John Fisher-Merritt in his garden of plenty.

A purple bell pepper.

Beets ready for harvest.

PHOTO OF JOHN BY JEFF PETCOFF

Desserts

LEFSE

When Ole was dying, his wife went to the kitchen and prepared several batches of her famous lefse.

"Lena," he called to her in his weak voice. "Can you bring me some of that lefse I love so much?"

"No," she replied. "It's for the funeral."

INGREDIENTS:

3 pounds riced potatoes

1 stick of melted butter

1 ½ tablespoons sugar

1 tablespoon salt

½ cup milk

2 ½ cups flour

DIRECTIONS:

* Peel potatoes and place them in boiling water. Boil until they are completely soft and break apart when pierced with a fork.

* Rice potatoes into a large mixing bowl.

* Mix flour, sugar and salt in a separate mixing bowl and add to the riced potatoes.

* Add milk and melted butter to the mix and combine together mixing by hand with a spoon. Do not over mix.

* Scoop dough balls that are about ¼ cup and roll out into thin round sheets using a rolling pin or press thin with your hands. Use a little flour if the dough is too sticky.

* Lift sheets off counter with a stick and roll onto large griddle that is about 400 degrees, or place into a non-stick pan.

* Cook until bubbles form and each side has browned.

* After lefse is cooked, place on a plate and cover with a damp paper towel to avoid drying out. Yields about 25 lefse.

BROWNIES

Brownies are a classic on their own, but also work well in more elaborate desserts. Try one with hot fudge sauce, vanilla ice cream, and whipped cream.

INGREDIENTS:

½ pound butter

2 cups sugar

2 teaspoons vanilla

4 eggs, room temperature

¾ cup cocoa powder, sifted if lumpy

1 cup all-purpose flour

½ teaspoon baking powder

¼ teaspoon salt

DIRECTIONS:

* Pre-heat oven to 350 degrees.

* Butter baking pan. Use a 9 x 9 inch pan if you want cakey brownies or a 9 x 13 inch pan if you want them moist and chewy.

* Melt butter and let cool. In a small mixer add butter, sugar, vanilla and mix well.

* While mixing, add eggs one at a time. Add cocoa powder and mix.

* Add flour, baking powder and salt.

* Mix together evenly. Batter will be heavy and dense.

* Pour batter into prepared pan.

* Bake for 25-45 minutes (depending on the size of pan used) or until a pick comes out clean.

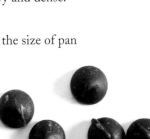

APPLE CRISP

Apple crisp is hearty and simple, the kind of fall classic that feels like it's been around forever. But the first recorded appearance in a cookbook is in 1924. It's a more efficient way to make apple pie, since instead of worrying about getting the perfect crust, you can throw a bunch of ingredients together and bake. It's also forgiving, since there aren't set rules on the proportion of topping to filling. So take heart, college students—if you're a little off on the quantities, it still tastes good. And isn't that's all that matters anyway?

INGREDIENTS:

Filling:

¾ cup sugar

1 tablespoon plus ¾ teaspoon kudzu

½ tablespoon salt

½ teaspoon cinnamon

¼ teaspoon nutmeg

5 tablespoons water

2 pounds frozen apples (about 6 cups sliced)

Topping:

1 cup flour

1 cup old fashioned oats

½ cup brown sugar (packed)

½ cup granulated sugar

6 ounces butter (room temp.)

DIRECTIONS:

- In a mixing bowl mix sugar, starch, salt, cinnamon and nutmeg.

- In another bowl add water to apples and mix until the water is used up. This will help the sugar mixture to adhere to the frozen apples. Toss apples with the sugar mixture.

- Grease a 9 X 13 inch pan.

- Add apples and sugar mixture to pan.

- In a separate bowl mix flour, oats, sugar and brown sugar. Cut in butter.

- Spread topping evenly over apples.

- Bake at 350 degrees for 1 ½ hours or until golden brown.

Note:

*If using fresh apples skip
using the water.*

CHEESECAKE

This delightful dessert has been with us since the ancient Greeks and is now found around the world. The Duluth Grill cheesecake is an example of the American New York style, which uses sour cream to create a richer, denser, cake.

INGREDIENTS:

Crust:

2 cups graham cracker crumbs

½ cup sugar

1 ¼ teaspoons cinnamon

¼ pound butter (1 stick), melted

Filling:

3 eggs

1 pound cream cheese (room temperature)

1 cup sugar

¼ teaspoon salt

2 tsp vanilla

3 cups sour cream (room temperature)

DIRECTIONS:

Crust:

- Mix together graham crackers, sugar, cinnamon and melted butter.
- Pour into an ungreased 9 inch spring form pan.
- Press into bottom and sides of pan to form a crust.

Filling:

- In a mixing bowl mix eggs.
- While still beating add cream cheese, sugar, salt, vanilla and sour cream.
- Mix well until smooth.
- Cover the outside of the spring form pan with aluminum foil.
- Pour filling into pan.
- Place spring form pan in a large roasting pan.
- Pour enough boiling water into roasting pan to come half-way up the sides of the spring form pan.
- Bake at 350 degrees for 60 - 70 minutes until a toothpick comes out clean.
- It should be a light golden brown around the edges.

Cheesecake Around the World

Many cultures have their own versions of a cheesecake. The first known cheesecakes come from Greece, where athletes would munch on a simple cake baked from flour, water, honey and cheese to fortify themselves for the games to come. The Romans took the recipe (along with everything else in Greece) and made it their own by adding eggs. Since that time, it's spread around the world, from dryer, more cake-like versions served in Germany to cheesecake served with guava marmalade in Brazil.

CREAM CHEESE FROSTING

The two sweetest words in the English language—"cream cheese" and "frosting"—come together beautifully in this topping.

INGREDIENTS:

1 pound cream cheese (room temperature)
5 cups powdered sugar
½ pound butter (room temperature)
2 teaspoons vanilla

DIRECTIONS:

- Mix all ingredients together with a mixing bowl.
- Mix until smooth and there are no chunks.
- Spread over cakes or muffins.

Note:

Instead of using this as a frosting, you could eat the entire mixture with a spoon. But we don't recommend it.

BANANA LAYER CAKE

Bananas can be quite healthy, but hey—haven't you had enough of all this "healthy" business for awhile? Tell the Diet Police to take a hike and dig in to bananas at their finest.

INGREDIENTS:

1 ½ cups All Purpose flour	¾ teaspoon baking powder
¾ teaspoon baking soda	¼ teaspoon salt
8 tablespoons butter, softened	¾ cups sugar
1 egg yolk	1 teaspoon vanilla
¾ cup banana puree	⅓ cup buttermilk
3 egg whites	

DIRECTIONS:

- Preheat oven to 350 degrees.
- Grease and flour a 9 inch, round cake pan.
- In a small bowl mix flour, baking powder, baking soda and salt. Set aside.
- Mix butter and sugar in mixer until fluffy, about 3 minutes.
- Beat in the egg yolk and vanilla.
- Add the bananas and mix until smooth.
- Add half of the dry ingredients and mix at low speed until batter is moistened.
- Mix in half of the buttermilk then add the remaining dry ingredients and remaining buttermilk.
- In a separate bowl beat the egg whites at medium-high speed until firm peaks form.
- Mix in one fourth of the egg whites into the batter at low speed.
- Using a rubber spatula, fold in the rest of the whites until no streaks remain.
- Scrape the batter into the prepared pan and smooth the top.
- Bake for 30-40 minutes at 350 degrees, until the top is golden and springy and a toothpick comes out clean.
- Cool in the pan for about 15 minutes then remove from pan and let cool completely.

PIE CRUSTS

If the pie crust recipe looks familiar, that's because it's the same as the recipe for the shell for pasties (page 102). This is a blind baked pie crust, which means it's baked before filling is added. The process creates a stronger crust that doesn't get soggy quickly when filled.

INGREDIENTS:

8-½ cups flour

3 cups shortening

1-½ tablespoons salt

3 eggs

2-¾ tablespoons white vinegar

1 cup ice cold water

DIRECTIONS:

- In a large mixing bowl, add the flour and salt and mix well.
- Add shortening to the flour and mix until flour has been absorbed by the shortening, leaving small marble sized chunks of shortening. Don't over mix.
- In a separate bowl, mix the eggs, vinegar and water. Mix well.
- Add the wet mix to the dry mix. Divide into 24 balls and roll out each one on a floured surface. Preheat oven to 350 degrees.
- Spray a large muffin tin (3 inch holes) with pan release spray. Form the pie crust to the tin by pressing it completely into the muffin tin, leaving a one inch rim around the top. Brush with an egg wash and sprinkle with sugar. Bake for seven to ten minutes.

Tip:

"I never mix the dough," Tom says. Instead, he gently mixes flour, shortening, and salt. Then, he stirs water, vinegar, and eggs together separately. He pours it into the flour, lifts from the bottom, set it on top, and pushes it down. (Basically pressing the liquid and flour-shortening mixture together.) "For us it creates a flaky crust every time," Tom says.

CREAM PIE FILLINGS

BANANA, COCONUT & VANILLA CREAM PIE FILLING

This sweet, creamy filling is terrific on its own, but also makes a good base for other toppings. To make a coconut cream pie, add toasted or fresh shredded coconut. To make a banana cream pie, line the crust with slices of one banana before filling.

INGREDIENTS:

1 ½ cups sugar

½ cup cornstarch

1 teaspoon salt

6 cups milk

6 egg yolks

¼ cup butter

2 teaspoons pure vanilla extract

DIRECTIONS:

- In a large saucepan add sugar, cornstarch and salt. Mix well.
- Mix in milk until smooth.
- Bring to a boil stirring occasionally.
- Boil for 2 minutes then turn heat off.
- Temper the yolks with about ½ cup of hot mix.
- Gradually pour the yolks back into pan stirring constantly.
- Let mixture come back to a boil and boil for 1 more minute.
- Add butter and vanilla, stir, and chill.

Yields about 1 ½ quarts. Good for a 10 inch pie.

Tip:

*Temper the eggs in a metal bowl. When the bowl
is too hot to hold, you
can dump it back in
the pudding.*

CHOCOLATE CREAM PIE FILLING

It's also known as French silk pie, but true patriots call it Chocolate Cream Pie. U-S-A! U-S-A!

INGREDIENTS:

1 ½ cups sugar

½ cup cornstarch

1 teaspoon salt

½ cup Dutch cocoa powder

6 cups milk

6 egg yolks

¼ cup butter

DIRECTIONS:

- In a large saucepan add sugar, cornstarch, salt and cocoa powder. Mix well.
- Mix in milk until smooth.
- Bring to a boil stirring occasionally.
- Boil for 2 minutes then turn heat off.
- Temper the yolks with about ½ cup of hot mix. Gradually pour the yolks back into pan stirring constantly.
- Let mixture come back to a boil and boil for 1 more minute.
- Add butter stir, and chill.

   Yields about 1 ½ quarts. Good for a 10 inch pie.

BLUEBERRY PIE FILLING

Picking wild blueberries is one of summer's inalienable delights, but this recipe works just as well with the frozen kind.

INGREDIENTS:

1 cup sugar

2 ¼ teaspoons salt

1 teaspoon cinnamon

6 cups frozen blueberries

5 ounces water

3 tablespoons kudzu (kuzu)

6 tablespoons cold water

DIRECTIONS:

- In a bowl mix sugar, salt and cinnamon.
- In a separate, large bowl mix berries with water, until frosty consistency.
- Add dry mix to blueberry mix. Mix well.
- Grease an oven proof pan. Add berries and cover with foil.
- Bake at 350 degrees for 1 hour.
- Remove from oven and strain juice from berries. You should have about 2 cups of juice.
- Place juice in saucepan.
- Mix kudzu with cold water mixing thoroughly to dissolve.
- Add to juice and boil gently, stirring constantly until thickened.
- Add fruit to thickened juice, stir and chill. Yields 4 cups.

APPLE PIE FILLING

Second only to baseball and mom, apple pie has forever earned its place in the pantheon of American culture.

INGREDIENTS:

1 ¼ cups sugar

1 ¼ teaspoons salt

¾ teaspoon cinnamon

½ teaspoon nutmeg

2 pounds frozen apples

½ cup water

2 ¼ tablespoons kuzu (kudzu)

4 ½ tablespoons cold water

DIRECTIONS:

- In a mixing bowl mix sugar, salt, cinnamon and nutmeg.

- In a separate bowl toss the apples with ½ cup of water until apples are coated.

- Pour the sugar mixture over the apples and toss until the apples are coated with the sugar mixture.

- Grease an oven proof pan. Add apples and cover with foil.

- Bake at 350 degrees for 1 hour.

- Remove from oven and strain juice from the apples. Should have about 1 ½ cups juice.

- Place juice in saucepan.

- Mix kuzu with cold water mixing thoroughly to dissolve.

- Add to juice and boil gently, stirring constantly until thickened.

- Add fruit to thickened juice, stir and chill. Yields about 4 cups.

LEMON PIE FILLING

When life gives you lemons, make this tangy dessert.

INGREDIENTS:

2 ½ cups sugar

¾ cup cornstarch

1 teaspoon salt

2 ½ cups water

1 cup lemon juice

6 egg yolks

¼ cup butter

1 tablespoon lemon zest

DIRECTIONS:

- In a medium saucepan combine sugar, cornstarch and salt. Mix well.

- Mix in water and lemon juice until smooth.

- Over medium heat bring mixture to a boil, stirring constantly.

- Remove from heat.

- Temper egg yolks with ½ cup of hot mixture.

- Gradually pour yolks back into pan while continuing to stir over medium heat.

- Bring to a boil for 1 more minute.

- Remove from heat and stir in butter and grated lemon zest.

- Stir until smooth and chill. Yields about 1 ½ quarts, good for a 10 inch pie.

CHOCOLATE CAKE & FROSTING

This makes a decadent chocolate layer cake—perfect for birthday cakes!

INGREDIENTS:

Cake:

2 ¼ cups sugar

2 cups + 2 tablespoons all purpose flour

1 cup cocoa powder-sifted to remove lumps

2 ½ teaspoons baking powder

1 ¾ teaspoons baking soda

1 ¾ teaspoons salt

2 eggs

1 cup milk

½ cup vegetable oil

2 teaspoons vanilla

1 cup boiling water

Frosting:

½ pound butter, melted

1 ⅓ cups cocoa powder-sifted

6 cups powdered sugar-sifted

⅔ cup milk

2 teaspoons vanilla

DIRECTIONS:

Cake:

- Preheat the oven to 350 degrees.
- Generously grease 2- 9 inch round pans and coat with cocoa powder.
- In a large mixing bowl combine dry ingredients.
- In a mixer bowl add eggs, milk, oil, and vanilla and mix at medium speed.
- Add dry ingredients to wet.
- Stir in the boiling water. (Batter will be thin)
- Pour evenly into prepared pans.

- Bake at 350 degrees for about 30-35 minutes or until a toothpick comes out clean.
- Cool in the pans for about 15 minutes before flipping cakes out of the pans.
- Let cool completely before frosting.

Frosting:

- In a mixer combine melted butter and cocoa.
- Alternately add powdered sugar and milk.
- Beat on medium speed to spreading consistency.
- Add more milk if too thick.
- Stir in vanilla.

Tip:

To ensure cake releases from pans line them with parchment paper before filling with batter. Do not ever *refrigerate the frosting. Once you refrigerate it, it sets, and will never spread again. You can get the layers cold in advance, but frost the cake immediately.*

CHOCOLATE CHIP COOKIES

When everyone from four year olds to ninety-four year olds loves something, there's probably a lot to love. Chocolate chip cookies are a great example.

INGREDIENTS:

1 cup shortening

¾ cup packed brown sugar

¾ cups granulated sugar

½ tablespoon plus ½ teaspoon vanilla extract

2 eggs

2 ¾ cups all purpose flour

½ tablespoon plus ¼ teaspoon baking soda

½ tablespoon plus ¼ teaspoon salt

¾ pound chocolate chips

DIRECTIONS:

* Preheat oven to 350 degrees.

* Cream shortening, sugar, brown sugar and vanilla extract; mix well.

* Add eggs to the mixture; mix well.

* In a separate bowl, mix flour, baking soda, and salt together; add to wet ingredients and mix well.

* Scoop heaping tablespoon sized scoops of dough onto a greased cookie sheet at least two inches apart.

* Bake at 350 degrees for 14-16 minutes. Yields 24 cookies.

Tip:

If you wonder if a cookie is done or not, you should be able to pick it up gently and look at the bottom. The bottom should be golden brown.

MOLASSES COOKIES

Go old-school with this sweet cookies, which get their depth from a liberal dose of molasses.

INGREDIENTS:

1 cup shortening

1 cup sugar

4 eggs

¾ cup molasses

¾ cup brown sugar

¾ tablespoon pure vanilla extract

3 ½ cup all-purpose flour

2 teaspoons baking soda

2 teaspoons salt

2 teaspoons cinnamon

4 cups oatmeal

2 cups raisins

DIRECTIONS:

* Preheat oven to 350 degrees.

* In a large mixing bowl, add the shortening, sugar, brown sugar, vanilla extract, eggs and molasses; mix well.

* In a separate bowl mix the flour, baking soda, salt, cinnamon and oatmeal; mix well.

* With the mixer on, slowly add the flour mixture to the molasses mixture; mix well.

* Add the raisins and mix well.

* Scoop heaping tablespoon sized scoops of dough onto a greased cookie sheet at least two inches apart.

  Bake at 350 degrees for 16-20 minutes. Yields 24 cookies.

PEANUT BUTTER COOKIES

Channel your inner George Washington Carver with yet another use for the peanut.

INGREDIENTS:

½ cup (1 stick) butter

½ cup shortening

1 cup peanut butter

1 cup plus 2 tablespoons granulated sugar

1 cup brown sugar

2 eggs

2 ½ cups all-purpose flour

1 ½ teaspoons baking soda

1 ½ teaspoons baking powder

1 teaspoon salt

DIRECTIONS:

- Preheat oven to 350 degrees.
- Cream butter, peanut butter, brown sugar and 1 cup granulated sugar.
- Beat in eggs.
- In a separate bowl, sift flour, baking soda, baking powder and salt. Stir into batter until blended.
- Refrigerate 1 hour
- Scoop heaping tablespoon sized scoops of dough onto a greased cookie sheet at least two inches apart.
- With a fork press down cookies in a criss cross pattern.
- Sprinkle with remaining sugar.

  Bake at 350 degrees for 14-16 minutes.
  Yields 24 cookies.

CHOCOLATE TRUFFLES

Truffles have a reputation for being fancy, but they could hardly be easier to make. A simple ganache of heavy cream and chocolate provides a base that can be customized with any kind of liqueur.

INGREDIENTS:

1 cup heavy cream

10 ounces bittersweet chocolate (chopped small)

3 tablespoons unsalted butter (cut small)

3 tablespoons liqueur of choice

14 ounces sweetened chocolate to coat

DIRECTIONS:

- Pour cream into a saucepan.
- Bring to a boil over medium heat. Remove from heat.
- Add chocolate and stir in the butter until melted.
- Stir in the liqueur.
- Strain into a bowl and cool to room temperature.
- Cover the mixture with plastic wrap and chill overnight.
- Line a large baking sheet with parchment paper.
- Shape truffles into balls using about 3 tablespoons for each. It helps to lightly wet your hands to do this.
- When coating with chocolate, freeze the balls for at least one hour.
- For perfect results temper the chocolate in a bowl over a low simmering pot of heated water.
- Using a fork dip the truffles, one at a time, into the melted chocolate, tapping the fork on the edge of the bowl to shake off the excess chocolate.
- Place on a lined baking sheet.
- If the chocolate begins to thicken reheat it gently until smooth.
- Chill the truffles until set. Makes about 20 truffles.

MEET OUR SUPPLIERS

Our suppliers really mean a lot to us. 33% of all of our food comes directly from small, local suppliers, and that number gets higher when you consider the fact that our large distributors often source locally as well. Here's a list of what we are working on. Expect it to grow over time.

- **Rain Forest Alliance Organic Coffee** – roasted and supplied locally from Alakef Coffee
- **Mountain Water Decaffeinated Coffee**
- Herbal Tea Blends from **Anahata Herbal Apothecary**
- **Fair Trade** – organic teas
- Cage-free organic eggs
- Organic salad greens
- Organic whole wheat & white flour
- Milk & cream in returnable bottles & butter from **Dahl's Sunrise Dairy** in Babbitt, MN
- All natural sour cream
- Hot cocoa made with real milk & organic dutch cocoa
- White fish from **Lake Superior Fish Company**
- Smoked salmon by Eric Goerdt at **Northern Waters Smokehaus**
- Organic produce from John Fisher-Merrit – **Food Farm**
- Organic produce from Rick & Karola Dalen from **Northern Harvest Farm**
- Organic produce, pickles, and jelly from Kathy Jensen – **Talmadge Farms**
- All grass fed beef burgers from Mark Thell – **4 Quarters Holdings**
- Bison from **Quarter Master Buffalo** in Esko
- Bison from Dave & Linda Majewski of Wisconsin
- Wild rice from Northern Minnesota
- **Lifeway Kefir** for kids
- Organic produce from the **UMD Farm**

- **Gerber Amish Chicken** – cage free, no chlorine wash, all vegetarian feed, antibiotic free
- Wild Alaskan salmon supplied by the Rogotzke Family
- Pure maple syrup harvested locally and supplied by the Rogotzke Family
- Honey from Ike Strohmayer – **Mirror Lake Beeworks**
- Honey from Marge & Don Korhonen – **Korhonen Apiaries**
- Organic bread & buns from **Positively 3rd Street Bakery**
- Tomatoes from **Bay Produce** in Superior, WI
- Cage free turkey from Thief River Falls, MN
- Duck from Christian Gasset – **Au Bon Canard** – Caledonia, MN
- Nitrate free all natural turkey breast
- Homemade caramel sauce, hot fudge, jams, peanut butter, ketchup, mustard and BBQ sauce
- Homemade vinaigrettes made simply with olive oil
- All natural lemonade made from lemons, water & sugar
- Our artwork has been purchased from local artists
- Our coffee mugs are locally made by Karin Kraemer at **Duluth Pottery**
- We offer health coverage to all employees working 16 hours a week minimum
- Spirit Lake wild rice harvested locally by Bruce Savage
- Fresh eggs supplied by Jason Amundson's **Locally Laid Egg Farm** in Wrenshall

ACKNOWLEDGEMENTS

There is nothing like putting together a cookbook to make you realize the enormous time, effort, and expense that goes into running a successful restaurant for even one day. So I want to start by thanking Tom and Jaima for running such a great restaurant, and for continuing to innovate. The last I talked to Tom, he was perfecting an Oaxacan-inspired molé and was puttering around with corn husks to develop tamales. You two inspire me as a food writer and I am continually impressed with the work you do.

I also want to thank the rest of the Duluth Grill team—Jeff, Louis, Don, Elliot, Dan and the front of house and back of house workers that make the restaurant a great place to visit.

Normally, this is where I would thank my publisher and editor. But since Tom is publishing the book and I'm editing the thing, I'll thank the other key people on this project. Rick, only you know how many hours you put into designing, redesigning, and re-re-designing our book. Rolf, without your beautiful photography, this book wouldn't be what it is. Amy and Brooke, thanks for all your work also. Ana Quincoces Rodriguez, we've only spoken once, but your cookbook ¡Sabor! inspired this book's look, feel, and casual tone. On my end, I have to thank my wife Alicia for her support and her eagle-eyed proofreading. And thanks for not using that same eagle-eyed discernment when you agreed to marry me.

Then there are those who helped on the cooking side. Darlene, Sarah, Kristina, and Angie, your help testing these recipes and translating them into the language of the home cook was invaluable. Jen, thanks so much for giving me guidance on what is gluten-free and what isn't (any mistakes are my own, not Jen's).

Since this is my first book, it's appropriate to thank those people who helped get me into food writing in the first place. Wendy Webb, you've been a good editor, and I appreciate your guidance over the years. To my high school English teachers Greg Jones and Sheryl Jensen, know that your classes made an impact on me to this day.

Finally, of course, I have to thank all the customers of the Duluth Grill. Without your avid, enthusiastic support, we would never have even started on a cookbook. In a sense, this book is really dedicated to you. May you get many years of pleasure from using it, and we'll see you at the Grill. **DG**

INDEX

D U L U T H G R I L L